EXPLORATION INTO INSIGHT

J. Krishnamurti

EXPLORATION INTO INSIGHT

HARPER & ROW, PUBLISHERS

SAN FRANCISCO

Cambridge
Hagerstown
Philadelphia
New York

1817

London
Mexico City
São Paulo
Sydney

Library of Congress Cataloging in Publication Data

Krishnamurti, Jiddu, 1895-
   Exploration into insight.

    1. Man—Addresses, essays, lectures.
2. Self (Philosophy)—Addresses, essays, lectures.
3. Perception—Addresses, essays, lectures.
4. Mind and body—Addresses, essays, lectures.
I. Title.
BD450.K697   1980   128′.2   79-6651
ISBN 0-06-064811-2

80 81 82 83 84 10 9 8 7 6 5 4 3 2 1

CONTENTS

LIST OF ABBREVIATIONS

K: Krishnaji   J. Krishnamurti
A: Achyut   Achyut Patwardhan
Apa: Apa Pant   Apa Pant
B: Balasundaram   S. Balasundaram
DS: David Shainberg   David Shainberg
D: Deshpande   P. Y. Deshpande
FW: Fritz Wilhelm   Fritz Wilhelm
GM: Ghaneshyam Mehta   Ghaneshyam Mehta
JC: John Coats   John Coats
KB: Kabir Bedi   Kabir Bedi
M: Maurice   Maurice Frydman
N: Nandini   Nandini Mehta
Par: Parchure   T. K. Parchure
PB: Parveen Babi   Parveen Babi
P: Pupul   Pupul Jayakar
Q: Questioner   Questioner
R: Radha   Radha Burnier
Raj: Rajesh Dalal   Rajesh Dalal
Rad: Radhika   Radhika Herzberger
S: Sunanda   Sunanda Patwardhan
SWS: Sundaram   S. W. Sundaram
VA: Vijay Anand   Vijay Anand

FOREWORD

These dialogues extend over a wide range of subjects. For over 30 years, a group of people from various disciplines, backgrounds and pursuits, deeply concerned with the enormity of the challenge facing humanity and with one central interest, the unfoldment of the self through the perceptive field of self-knowledge, have gathered around J. Krishnamurti to undertake together, through dialogue, the investigation of the structure and nature of man's mind and consciousness and the energy resources that lie dormant within man's being. The concern in these dialogues is the freedom of the mind from the bondages of memory and time, a mutation in consciousness and the arising of insight that gives deep roots of steadiness to the mind.

In the world today, scientific and technological revolution has unharnessed undreamt-of resources of power and knowledge. However, man has failed to discover in himself the sources of wisdom and compassion. What is needed is an inner revolution in the psyche of man. The insight that man lacks is the apprehension that he is the maker of his problems and that the root of this problem-making machinery is his mind. It is in this area of perception that the ultimate freedom of man lies.

Starting tentatively, there is in these dialogues a relentless questioning, probing and inquiry, a 'listening' and a 'seeing' in which depths of the self with its vast subtleties and hidden escapes are exposed. This exploration to Krishnamurti is 'a journey into time, into the past, into the limitless'.

Man caught in the paradox of living, rarely questions. He escapes from his anguish, his loneliness, his sorrow. In a world sated with sensations, man turns to the guru, to the religious experience, or extra-sensory powers that arise from various forms of concentration, as a further stimulus to his jaded appetites. Krishnamurti's teaching negates the guru and the psychic experience as a way to liberation. He demands a 'life of correctness', a daily life free from all self-centred activity. All psychic experiences as they arise have to be put aside for they can become obstacles and traps to insight, which alone frees man from duality and the bondage of time as the past.

Krishnamurti's rôle in these dialogues is of great interest. The dialogues are not questions and answers. Krishnamurti's mind is tentative, pliable, learning, seeking, probing; it is questioned, it pauses, observes, withdraws, to move forward again. There is no exchange of opinion, no spilling out of the verbal, no operation of memory as past experience, blocking the new. There is a listening with 'the total flowering of the senses'. In that intensity of enquiry, insight arises. Speaking of the nature of this state, Krishnamurti says 'there is only perception and nothing else. Everything else is movement in time. Perception is without time. There is a momentum which is timeless.'

The Krishnamurti Foundation India is offering these dialogues to those who seek fundamental answers to the problems of life.

PUPUL JAYAKAR
SUNANDA PATWARDHAN

Self-knowledge and the Teaching

P: What is the relationship between your teaching, as expressed in the words you use in your books and in your talks, and the actual process of self-knowing? In all other ways of arriving at truth, the words of the teacher are taken as an indication of a direction, something to move towards. Are your words of the same nature and, if so, what is their relationship to the perceptive process of self-knowing?

K: I wonder whether I have understood the question. Am I right if I put it this way: What is the relationship between the word and the actuality that K is talking about? Is that it?

P: When K talks about discipline, or talks about the holistic approach, that is the word. Then there is the actual process of self-knowing and what is revealed in self-knowing. What is the relationship of K's word to this revealed knowing?

K: I don't quite catch this.

P: You say 'no authority', no psychological or spiritual authority. We have a tendency to take that expression 'no authority' and apply it to our lives; which is, not be in that state, not discover freedom from authority in the process of self-knowing, but simply to try to see whether we can reach a state of non-authority. We take your word as the truth.

K: I understand. 'No authority,' is it an abstraction of words and therefore an idea and then one pursues that idea? When K says 'no authority', is it self-revealing, or is it merely a conclusion, a slogan?

A: There is also another side: when you say 'no authority', does it become a commandment, a commandment to which one tries the nearest approximation?

Kt: Yes, that's right.

A: One is in the field of action, and the other is in the field of abstraction.

P: There is self-knowing; that which is revealed in the process of self-knowing is not knowable through the word. One hears you speak, one takes in what you say, or one reads your books and applies it to one's daily life; therefore there is a gap between self-knowing and your word. Now, where does truth lie?

K: Neither in the word nor in the self-revealing. It is completely apart.

P: Can we discuss that?

K: I listen to K and he talks about self-knowing and lays emphasis on self-knowing, how important it is, that without self-knowing there is no foundation. He says this. I listen to it. In what manner do I listen to that statement? Do I listen to it as an idea, a commandment, a conclusion? Or is it that in my self-knowing, I realize the implications of authority and therefore see that what he says tallies with what I discover for myself? If I listen to the word and draw a conclusion about that word as an idea and pursue the idea, then it is not self-revealing. It is merely a conclusion. But when I am studying myself, when I am pursuing my own thoughts, then in the words of K there is a self-discovery?

P: Now, is the word of K necessary to self-discovery?

K: No. I make a statement: without self-knowing whatever I think whatever I do or proceed with, has no basis. So I come to talk or read a book because I am interested in self-knowing and I pursue that. And when I hear K talking about 'no authority', what is the state of my mind when I hear those words? Is it one of acceptance, is it a conclusion which I draw, or is it a fact?

P: How does it become a fact? Does it become a fact through the discovery of that in the perceptive process of self-knowing? Or is it a fact because you have said so?

12

K: The microphone is a fact. It is not because I say it is the microphone.

P: But when you say 'microphone', it is not a fact in the same sense as the microphone is a fact.

K: So, the word is not the thing. The description is not that which is described. So, am I clear on that point, that the word is never the thing? The word 'mountain' is not the mountain. Am I clear on that? Or is the description good enough for me and I get entangled in the description? Do I accept the description wanting that which is described and clinging to the idea? Don't reject the verbal structure altogether. I use language to communicate; I want to tell you something. I use words which we both know. But we both know that the words we use are not the actual feeling which I have. So the word is not the thing.

D: One talks either through the mental process or one talks without the mental process.

K: Sir, they are two different points. Either you communicate through the word or you communicate without the word.

D: No, words are there; but when we listen to you, we know you are not talking the way we talk.

K: Why do you say that?

D: It is a difficult question, but it is a definite feeling as factual as seeing a microphone. K is not talking the way I talk, the source of his words lies much deeper than the words we use.

K: I understand, sir. I can say superficially, 'I love you', but I can also say 'I really love you'. It is quite a different thing—the tone, the quality of the word, the depth of the feeling. The words convey the depth.

D: I will go a little further.

K: Go further.

D: They really convey a deep feeling which is indefinable, which we call love—but I do not know the word for it.

K: You may not know the word, yet I may hold your hand, I may make a gesture.

D: That's true. But now between the gesture and the word, there is no linkage.

K: Is that what you are trying to convey, Pupul?

P: One of our difficulties, in understanding and going beyond, is that one takes your word, either the spoken word or the written word, and it becomes an abstraction to which one approximates. Then, on the other hand, there is the process of self-knowing in which the truth of your word can be revealed; but it does not normally happen that way. It always seems to me that listening to you without obstacle may bring about a change in the nature of my mind as such, but the discovery of the actuality of the words you use, can only be revealed in the process of self-knowing.

K: What am I to say to that?

P: Sir, I think first of all we should investigate self-knowing. We have not done it for a very long time.

K: Let us do that. 'Self-knowing' was being spoken about, thousands of years ago, by Socrates and by others before him. Now, what is self-knowing? How do you know yourself? What is it to know oneself? Do you know yourself from the observation of experience; from the observation of a thought and from that thought the observation of another thought springing up, and we are reluctant to let go the first thought, so that there is a conflict between the first thought and the second thought? Or is self-knowing to relinquish the first thought and pursue the second thought and then the third thought that arises dropping the second, following the third; dropping the third and following the fourth; so that there is a constant alertness and awareness of the movement of thought? Now, let's proceed. I observe myself being jealous. The instinctual response to jealousy is rationalization. In the process of rationalization I have forgotten, or put aside, jealousy. So I am caught in rationalization, in words, in the capacity to examine and then to suppress. I see the whole movement as one unit. Then arises the desire to run away from it. I examine that desire, that escape. It is an escape into what?

P: Sometimes escape into meditation.

K: Of course, that is the easier trick—into meditation. So, I say, what is meditation? Is it an escape from 'what is'? Is that meditation? It is not meditation, if it is an escape. So, I go back and examine my jealousy: why am I jealous? because I am attached, because I think I am important and so on. This whole process is revelation. Then I come to the point: Is the examiner, the observer, different from the observed? Obviously he is not. So true observation is when there is no observer.

P: You said, 'Obviously he is not'. Let us go into that.

K: The observer is the past; he is the past, the remembrance, the experience, the knowledge stored up in memory. The past is the observer and I observe the present which is my jealousy, my reaction. And I use the word 'jealousy' for that feeling because I recognize it as having happened in the past. It is a remembrance of jealousy through the word which is part of the past. So, can I observe without the word and without the observer which is the past? Does the word bring that feeling or is there feeling without the word? All this is part of of self-knowledge.

P: How does one observe without the word?

K: Without the observer, without a remembrance. That is very important.

P: How does one actually tackle the problem of the observer?

A: May I say that in the watching of the observer, there is also the disapproval or the approval of the observer of himself.

K: That is the past. That is his conditioning. That is the whole movement of the past, which is contained in the observer.

A: That condemnation is the barrier.

K: That is what Pupul is asking. She says: How do I observe the observer? What is the process of observing the observer? I hear **K** say that the observer is the past. Is that so?

Par: In asking such a question, another observer is created.

K: No, I do not create anything. I am merely observing. The question is, what is the observer?—who is the observer? How do I observe this microphone? I observe it through a word that we have used to indicate that it is a microphone; it is registered in the brain as a microphone, as remembrance; I use that word to convey the fact of the microphone. That's simple enough.

P: Does one observe the observer?

K: I am coming to that. How does one observe the observer? You don't.

P: Is it the inability to observe the observer which gives one the understanding of the nature of the observer?

K: No. You do not observe the observer. You only observe 'what is' and the interference of the observer. You say you recognize the observer. You see the difference? Just go slowly. There is jealousy. The observer comes in and says: 'I have been jealous in the past; I know what that feeling is.' So I recognize it and it is the observer. You cannot observe the observer by itself. There is the observation of the observer only in its relationship to the observed. When the observer arrests the observation, then there is awareness of the observer. You cannot observe the observer by itself. You can only observe the observer in relation to something. That is fairly clear. At the moment of feeling there is neither the observer nor the observed, there is only that state. Then the observer comes in and says, that is jealousy and he proceeds to interfere with that which is, he runs away from it, suppresses it, rationalizes it, justifies it, or escapes from it. Those movements indicate the observer in relation to that which is.

FW: At the moment when the observer exists, is there a possibility of observation of the observer?

K: That is what we are saying. I am angry or violent. At the

16

moment of violence there is nothing. There is neither you the observer nor the observed. There is only that state of violence. Then the observer comes in which is the movement of thought. Thought is the past—there is no new thought—and that movement of thought interferes with the present. That interference is the observer and you study the observer only through that interference. It tries to escape from what is irrational in violence, to justify it and so on, which are all traditional approaches to the present. The traditional approach is the observer.

P: In a sense, therefore, the observer manifests itself only in terms of escaping from the present.

K: Escapes, or rationalizations.

D: Or interference.

K: Any form of interference with the present is the action of the observer. Don't accept this. Tear it to pieces, find out.

Par: If there is no past, is there no interference?

K: No, that is not the point. What is the past?

Par: The accumulated, stored contents of my experience.

K: Which is what? Your experiences, your inclinations and motives, all that is the movement of the past, which is knowledge. Movement of the past can only take place through knowledge, which is the past. So the past interferes with the present; the observer comes into operation. If there is no interference, there is no observer, there is only observation.

In observation there is neither the observer nor the idea of observation. This is very important to understand. There is neither observer nor the idea of not having an observer; which means there is only pure observation without the word, without the recollection and association of the past. There is nothing, only observation.

FW: In that way is the observation of the observer possible?

K: No, I said: The observation of the observer comes only when

17

the past interferes. The past is the observer. When that past interferes with the present, the observer is in action. It is only then that you become aware that there is an observer. Now, when you see that, when you have an insight into that, then there is no observer, there is only observation.

So can I observe 'no authority' *per se*, not because you have told me?

P: No, I can only observe one thing: the movement of authority. I can never observe 'no authority'.

K: Of course not. But there is the observation of authority; the observation of authority which is in the demand from another for enlightenment; the leaning on, the attachment to, another, all that is a form of authority. And is there 'authority' in operation in my brain, in my mind, in my being? 'Authority' may be experience, knowledge depending on the past—a vision and so on. Is there an observation of the movement of thought as 'authority'?

P: What is important? Is it the observation of every movement of my human mind, of my consciousness, or is it the attempt to discover in my consciousness the truth, the actuality of what you are saying? It is a very subtle thing. I do not know how to put it.

S: Can I put it this way? For instance, I observe hurt.

K: Do you observe hurt because K said it?

S: I see that I am hurt. I see the emergence of hurt. The observation of the hurt is something which I can do as part of self-knowing. But where do I create authority? When Krishnaji says: 'Once you see hurt it is over,' it is then that I create authority. Then I project a certain state, a movement towards that state, because I do not want to be caught in the trap of constant observation of hurt. But there are several other factors in consciousness. I see that instead of the observation of hurt, I hear from time to time a person saying that the observation of the hurt without the observer is the ending of hurt. That is where I create authority.

K: I understand. I observe the hurt and all the consequences of the hurt, how that hurt has come into being and so on. I am aware

18

of the whole process of that hurt and in my mind I hear **K** saying, once you see that in its entirety, holistically, then it is over, you will never be hurt. He has said that.

S: It is there in my consciousness.

K: What is in your consciousness? The word?

S: Apart from the word, the state which he communicated when he uttered that, because when **K** is talking, he seems to indicate a 'state' beyond the word.

K: Sunanda, look: I am hurt. I know I am hurt. By listening to you I see the consequences of all that—the withdrawal, the isolation, the violence, all that I see. Do I see it because you have pointed it out to me? Or do I see it though you have pointed it out to me?

S: Obviously the fact is there, you have come into my life and I have listened to you.

K: Then the question arises; **K** says once you see it fully, holistically, then the whole hurt is over. Where is the authority there?

S: Authority is there because it affirms a state which I would like to have.

K: Then examine that state which is ambition, which is desire.

P: I would like to examine your use of the word 'holistic' and also enquire into something you have said, which is: Can you hold hurt and remain with it—that is, holistically? What is involved in holding?

K: I am hurt. I know why I am hurt. I am aware of the image that is hurt and the consequences of that hurt—the escape, the violence, the narrowness, the fear, the isolation, the withdrawal, the anxiety, and all the rest of it. How am I aware of it? Is it because you have pointed it out to me? Or I am aware of it, I see it and I am moving with you? In that there is no authority. I am not separate from what you are saying. That's where the catch is.

S: Up to a point there is movement with you.

K: I am moving with you.

D: So your word is like a pointer.

K: No, no.

S: So long as I am moving with you, there is a relationship.

K: The moment I break that relationship, then begins my question: How am I to do it? If I am following exactly what you are saying—seeing that the image is hurt and then the escape, the violence—I am moving with you. It is like an orchestra, an orchestra of words, an orchestra of feeling, the whole thing is moving. As long as I am moving with you, there is no contradiction. Then you say 'Once you see this as a whole, the thing is over—am I with you?

S: It has not happened.

K: I will tell you why. Because you have not listened.

S: You mean to say that I have not listened for twenty years?

K: It doesn't matter. One day is good enough. You have not listened. You are listening to the word, and you are carrying along the reaction. You are not moving with him.

R: Is there a difference between that listening and the holistic view?

K: No. Listen. Can you listen in the sense of no interpretation, no examination, no comparison?

R: No expectation.

K: Nothing, just listening. I am listening. It is like two rivers moving together there as one river. But I do not listen that way. I have heard you say 'holistically' and I want to get that. Therefore I am no longer listening because I want that.

R: Therefore, the question of how to remain with whatever is, is a wrong question, isn't it?

K: I am remaining with it.

R: Yes, but the question itself is a movement away from remaining with it.

K: Of course.

P: There is a feeling of intensity of sorrow and an observation to see that this sorrow is not dissipated by any movement away from it. In a moment of crisis there is an intensity of energy and to remain with it totally, the only action is the refusal to move away from it. Is that valid?

R: Does it not mean that one can only watch every movement which is away from it and not to say how am I to remain with it?

P: Sorrow arises and it fills you. That is the way it operates when it is something very deep. What is the action on that? What is the action that will enable it to flower without dissipation?

K: If it fills you, actually, if your whole being is filled with that extraordinary energy called sorrow and there is no escape; but the moment you move away in any direction, it is a dissipation of that energy. Are you filled with that energy which is called sorrow completely, or is there a part of you, somewhere in you, where there is a loophole?

R: I think there is always a loophole because there is a fear of anything filling one's whole being. I think that fear is there.

K: So, sorrow has not filled your being.

R: No, that is so.

K: That is a fact. So you pursue not sorrow but fear. The fear what might happen, etc. So you go into that, you forget sorrow and go into that.

D: The use of the word 'holistic' implies actuality. Actuality itself is the whole.

K: No, no. Sir, let us understand the meaning of the word 'holistic'. Whole means healthy, physically healthy. Then it means sanity, mentally and physically and from that arises holy. All that is implied in the word 'holistic' or 'whole'.

D: This is clear for the first time.

K: When you have very good health and when the brain emotionally, intellectually, is sane without any quirk, without any neurotic movement, it is holy. That is the holistic approach. If there is a quirk, an idiosyncrasy, a belief, it is not whole—so clean it up, do not talk about holistic. The holistic happens when there is sanity, health.

S: This is where the dilemma comes. Pursue the fragment you say. But unless one sees the fragment holistically . . .

K: Do not bother about holistically.

S: Then, how does one observe the fragment? Then, what is the process involved? Which comes first?

K: I am doing it. I do not know a thing about holistic. I do not know. I know the meaning of the word, the description of the word, what it conveys, but that is not the fact. The fact is that I am a fragment, I work, live, act in fragments, in myself. I know nothing about the other.

FW: This brings us to the initial question: What is the meaning of your word apart from our communication now? In my daily life, to remember what you say that you should never be hurt, has it a meaning when I am hurt?

K: No, I am hurt. That is all I know. That is a fact. I am hurt because I have an image about myself. Have I discovered that image for myself or has K told me that the image is hurt? That is very important to find out. Is it that the description has created the image or is it that I know the image exists?

S: One knows that the image exists.

K: All right. If the image exists, I am concerned with the image, not how to be rid of the image, not how to look at the image holistically. I know nothing about it.

S: 'Looking at the image,' it seems to imply the concept of 'holistic'.

K: No, I know nothing of such concept. I only know I have an image. I will not be with anything but the fragment, with 'what is'—the holistic is non-fact.

S: That is very clear. But how does one look at it, hold the hurt *totally*? That is where the question arises.

P: That is his statement.

K: What?

S & P: 'Totally.' That is your statement.

K: Of course. But throw it out.

S: Then there is no problem because one observes certain symptoms of hurt. There is an observation of it and it ends. This process goes on, I do not need K's telling me about it. This I know; to observe something at that level, everything that is arising in consciousness, the observing of it and the subsidence.

A: The discussion started on the very crucial question of authority. The point of starting this discussion on authority lies in this, that we make an authority of what you have said, then that is a barrier.

K: Obviously.

D: Something is missing in this.

K: Look, sir, there is something very interesting which comes out of this. Are you learning or are you having an insight into it? Learning implies authority. Are you learning and acting from learning? I learn about mathematics, technology and so on and from that knowledge I become an engineer and act. Or I go out into the field, act and learn. Both are the accumulation of knowledge and acting from knowledge—knowledge becomes the authority. Either you accumulate knowledge and act or you go out, act and learn. Both are an acting according to knowledge. So knowledge becomes the authority, whether it is the authority of the doctor, the scientist, the architect, or the guru who says 'I know'—which is his authority. Now, somebody comes along and says: 'Look, acting according to knowledge is a prison; you will never be free; you can not ascend through knowledge.' And somebody like K says: 'Look at it differently, look at action with insight—not accumulate knowledge and act but insight and action. In that there is no authority.

P: You have used the word 'insight'. What is the actual meaning of that word?

K: To have insight into something; to grasp the thing instantly; to listen carefully. You see, you do not listen, that is my point. You act, after learning; that is, in learning there is an accumulation of information, knowledge and you act according to that knowledge, skilfully or non-skilfully. That is learning; accumulating knowledge and acting from it. Then there is learning from acting, which is the same as the other. Both are acting on the basis of knowledge. So knowledge becomes the authority and where there is authority there must be suppression. You will never ascend anywhere through that process; it is mechanical. Do you see both as mechanical movement? If you see that, that is insight. Therefore, you are acting not from knowledge; but by seeing the implications of knowledge and authority. Your action is totally different.

So where are we? Self-knowledge and the word of K. If there is a movement together, then it is over. It is very simple. You move.

P: Is the word of K and the movement with that word essential? Can the revelation be without the word?

K: All right. K says: 'Be a light to yourself.' It does not mean you become the authority. K says: 'Nobody can take you there; you can not invite that.' K says: 'You can listen to K endlessly for the next million years and you will not get it.' But he says: 'Be a light to yourself' and you see holistically that thing. To know oneself is one of the most difficult things because in the observation of myself I come to a conclusion about what I am seeing; and the next observation is through that conclusion. Can one observe the actual anger without any conclusion, without saying right, wrong, good, bad? Can one observe holistically? Self-knowledge is not knowing oneself, but knowing every movement of thought. Because the self

24

is the thought, the image, the image of K and the image of the 'me'
So, watch every movement of thought, never letting one thought go without realizing what it is. Try it. Do it and you will see what takes place. This gives muscle to the brain.

S: Would you say that in a single thought is the essence of the self?

K: Yes. I will say 'yes'. You see, thought is fear, thought is pleasure, thought is sorrow. And thought is not love. Thought is not compassion.

The image that thought has created is 'me'. The 'me' is the image. There is no difference between 'me' and the image. The image is me. Now, I am observing the image which is me, which is, say, 'I want to attain nirvana,' which means I am greedy. That is all. Instead of wanting money, I want the other thing. It is greed. So I examine greed. What is greed? 'The more'? That means I want to change what is into the more, the greater. Therefore that is greed. So I say: 'Now why am I doing this?' 'Why do I want more?' Is it tradition, habit, is it the mechanical response of the brain? I want to find out. Either I can find out with one glance or step by step. I can observe it with one glance only when I have no motive, for motive is the distorting factor. It is most interesting to know yourself because yourself may be the universe—not the theoretical universe but the global universe. I want to know myself because I see very clearly that if I do not know myself, whatever I say is meaningless, is corrupt—not just verbally, I *see* that it is corruption. My action is corrupt action and I do not want to live a corrupt life. I see I must know myself. To know myself I watch; I watch my relationship to you, to my wife, to my husband. In that watching I see myself reflected in that relationship. I want my wife because I want sex; I want her comfort; she looks after my children; she cooks; I depend on her. So, in my relationship to her, I discover the pleasure principle, the attachment principle and the comfort principle and so on. Am I observing it without the past, without any conclusion? Is my observation precise? The moment one says 'Be a light to yourself', all authority is gone including the authority of the *Gita*, the gurus, the ashramas. The question would be really interesting on its own. If I am a light to myself, what is my relationship

25

politically, economically, socially? But you do not ask these questions. I am a light to myself—go on, work it out—I am a light to myself. I see that very clearly. I have no authority, no guide. Then how do I act with regard to tyranny, the tyranny of the guru, of the ashramas? To be a light to oneself means being holistic. Anything that is not holistic is corruption. A holistic man will not deal with corruption.

The Ending of Recognition

P: Shall we discuss the question of consciousness and the relationship of consciousness to the brain cells? Are they of the same nature or is there something which gives them separate identities?

K: That's a good question. You begin.

P: The traditional concept of the word 'consciousness' would include that which lies beyond the horizon.

A: Quite correct. The brain is only a conglomeration of cells, a forest of cells and yet each cell is dependent on the other although in fact every brain cell can act by itself. So we may ask: How does one know the sum total of all consciousness, of all the cells? Is there a co-ordinating factor? Is the brain merely a result? A further question is: What is primary and what secondary? Does consciousness come first and then the brain, or does the brain come first and then consciousness?

K: If I may ask: What do you mean by the word 'consciousness'? Let us start from the beginning: What is consciousness? What does it mean 'to be conscious of'? I want to be clear that we both have the same understanding of the meaning of that word. One is conscious, for instance, of the microphone. I am conscious of it and then I use the word 'microphone'. So, when you are conscious of something naming begins; then like and dislike. So 'consciousness' means to be aware of, to be conscious of, to be cognisant of sensation, cognition, contact.

A: I feel that consciousness is prior to sensation. It is the field and at any one time I am aware of some part of it through sensation; I feel consciousness is much more vast. I see that I am aware of only a part of a very wide thing. That whole field is not in my awareness.

So, I do not want to restrict consciousness to something that exists at any given moment. My awareness may not be extensive, but consciousness can be seen to be much more vast.

K: What is the relationship between that consciousness and the brain cells? Pupul used the word 'consciousness' and asked what is the relationship between the brain and consciousness. I am asking: What is that relationship?

P: When K says the content of consciousness is consciousness, it would imply that the content of the brain cells is consciousness. If there is a field which is outside the brain cells and which is also consciousness, then you have to say all that is consciousness. But then you cannot say that the content of consciousness is consciousness.

K: Is that clear? I have said the content of consciousness is consciousness.

A: 'The content of consciousness is consciousness' is a statement irrespective of, and unconnected with, the perceiver. It is a statement about consciousness, not your consciousness, or my consciousness.

K: That is right. Therefore what is outside the field of consciousness is not its content.

P: The moment you posit something outside of consciousness, you are positing a state which may or may not exist.

A: Is the known a part of our consciousness, consciousness being the content?

P: The major difference between K's position and the Vedantic position is that K uses the word 'consciousness' in a very special sense. The Vedantic position is: consciousnesss is that which exists before anything exists.

A: Basically, the source of existence is a vast incomprehensible energy which they call 'Chaitanya'. 'Chaitanya' is the energy, the source. They say that there is this source of energy, which they speak of as 'Chit'. The Buddhist position does not say anything about this at all. It refuses to say a word about it. Therefore, the Buddhist position is one from which we cannot answer the enquiry. The Buddhist will say: 'Don't talk about it; any talk about it will be speculative and speculative processes are not meant for actual practice.'

K: 'Ignorance has no beginning, but has an end. Don't enquire into the beginning of ignorance but find out how to end it'.

A: We have immediately come upon something.

K: Right, sir, that's a good point.

A: Buddhists say: 'There is no such thing as consciousness in general. Ignorance has no beginning. Ignorance can end. Don't let us investigate into the beginnings of ignorance because that would be speculative, would be a waste of time. But how is it possible to end ignorance? This ignorance is consciousness.' Consciousness as ignorance is a position into which we will have to investigate.

The Vedantins will say to you that the source which you refer to as ignorance is of the nature of Sat, Chit and Anand. It is constantly renewing itself; it is constantly coming into being; and the entire process of birth, death, decay is a movement in it. I feel that a man who does not accept the Buddhist position, will not immediately accept what you say, that the beginning is ignorance and that it is a self-sustaining process. You cannot trace the beginning, but it can be brought to an end. I have stated the two positions and they are conflicting positions.

K: We simply say that ignorance has no beginning; one can see it in oneself, see it within consciousness, within that field.

P: If it is within this field, then has it existence apart from the brain cells which contain the memory about it? The scientific position is: whereas the brain cells and their operation are measurable, consciousness is not measurable and therefore the two are not synonymous.

K: Wait a minute. What you are saying is that the brain cells and their movement are measurable, but consciousness is not measurable.

A: May I suggest something? When we look through the biggest telescope, we see the expanse of the cosmos as far as that instrument will show it. If we get a bigger instrument, we get a bigger view. Though we measure it, that measurement is relevant only to the instrument which is a relative element. Consciousness is immeasurable in the sense that there is no instrument to which it can be related. Consciousness is something about which one cannot say that it is measurable or immeasurable. Therefore, consciousness is something about which one cannot make any statement.

K: That is right. Consciousness is not measurable. What Pupul is asking is: Is there outside consciousness as we know it, a state which is not pertinent to this consciousness?

P: Is there a state which is not divisible, not knowable, not available, within the brain cells?

K: Have you got it Achyutji? Not knowable, in the sense, not recognizable; something totally new.

A: I am coming to that. I say that consciousness as we know it is the source of all the recent memories and all the memories man has had. The brain cells will recognize everything that comes out of racial memories; everything that comes within the field of the past, out of that which has been known.

P: The millions of years of the known.

A: Even the earliest memories of man, the brain may be able to remember.

K: Wait, keep it very simple. We said the known is consciousness—the content of consciousness is the known. Now, is there something outside this, something which is not known, totally new and which does not already exist in the brain cells? If it is outside the known, is it recognizable?—for if it is recognizable it is still in the field of the known. It is available only when the recognizing

30

and experiencing process comes to an end. I want to stick to this. Pupul asked: Is it in the known or outside the known; and if it is outside the known, is it already in the brain cells? If it is in the brain cells, it is already the known because the brain cells cannot contain something new. The moment it is in the brain cells, it is tradition.

I love to dig deep. Outside the brain, is there anything else? That is all. I say there is. But every process of recognition, experience, is always within the field of the known and any movement of the brain cells moving away from the known, trying to investigate into the other is still the known.

M: How do you know that there is something?

K: You cannot *know* it. There is a state where the mind does not recognize anything. There is a state in which recognition and experience, which are the movement of the known, totally come to an end.

A: In what way is it differentiated from a state of the process of recognition, experiencing?

P: Is it of a different nature?

K: You see, the organism, the brain cells, come to an end. The whole thing collapses; there is a different state altogether.

P: Let me put it to you in another way. When you say that all the processes of recognition come to an end, and yet it is a living state, is there a sense of existence, of being?

K: The words, 'existence' and 'being' do not apply.

A: How is it different from deep sleep?

K: I don't know what you mean by deep sleep.

A: In deep sleep the processes of recognition and recording are for the time being put in total abeyance.

K: That is quite a different thing.

P: What has happened to the senses in the state you mentioned earlier?

31

K: The senses are in abeyance.

P: Are they not operating?

K: In that state, I might scratch myself—you follow—flies come and sit on me. That is the action of the senses, but it does not affect that.

M: The knowledge that there is scratching going on is present.

K: That is a natural thing. You must go very very slowly with it. Any movement of the known, any movement, potential or non-potential, is within the field of the known. I want to be quite clear that you and I are understanding the same thing. That is: when the content of consciousness with its experiences, demands, its craving for something new, including its craving for freedom from the known, has completely come to an end, then only does the other quality come into being. The former has a motive; the latter has no motive. The mind cannot come to that through motive. Motive is the known. So, can the mind come to an end which says: 'It is no good investigating into it, I know how to make it come to an end, ignorance is part of the content, ignorance is part of this demand to experience more?' When that mind comes to an end—an end not brought about by conscious effort in which there is motive, will, direction—then the other thing is there.

M: The thing is there. In the situation in which we are now, do you know that?

K: Of course, I see your shirt, I see the colour obviously. The senses are in operation. Recognition is in operation normally. The other is there. It is not a duality.

M: Is knowledge a part of it?

K: No. I must go very slowly. I know what you are getting at. I want to come to this very simply. I see the colour; the senses are in operation. . .

A: Even trying to translate what you are saying is preventing one from getting at it because that would immediately be duality.

When you say something, any movement in the mind is again preventing one from it.

K: Achyutji, what are you trying to get at?

A: I am pointing out the difficulty that arises in communication. I think communication about the other is not possible. I am trying to understand the conscious state of the mind of the man who talks to me. On what basis does he tell me that there is something?

K: The basis for that is: when there is no movement of recognition, of experiencing, of motive, freedom from the known takes place.

M: That is pure cognition without recognition.

K: You are translating it differently. This movement has come to an end for the time being; that is all.

M: The movement of recognition of that. Where does the time element come in? Is there another time?

K: Let us begin again. The brain functions within the field of the known; in that function there is recognition. But when the brain, your mind, is completely still, you don't see your still mind. There is no knowing that your mind is still. If you know it, it is not still, for then there is an observer who says 'I know'. The stillness which we are talking about is non-recognizable, non-experienceable. Then comes along the entity that wants to tell you this through verbal communication. The moment he, the entity, moves into communication, the still mind is not. Just look at it. Something comes out of it. It is there for man. I am not saying it is always there. It is there for the man who understands the known. It is there and it never leaves; and though he communicates it, he feels that it is never gone, it is there.

M: Why do you use the word 'communicate'?

K: That is communication.

M: Who communicates? You talked to me just now.

K: Just now? The brain cells have acquired the knowledge of the language. It is the brain cells that are communicating.

M: The brain contains its own observer.

K: The brain itself is the observer and the operator.

M: Now what is the relationship between that and this?

K: Tentatively, I say there is no relationship. This is the fact: the brain cells hold the known and when the brain is completely stable, completely still, there is no verbal statement or communication—the brain is completely still. Then, what is the relationship between the brain and that?

M: By what magic, by what means, does the state of a still mind make a bridge? How do you manage to make a permanent bridge between the brain and that, and maintain that bridge?

K: If one says 'I don't know', what will you answer?

M: You have inherited it through some karma or somebody has given it to you.

K: Let us begin again. Is it by chance that that event can happen to us, is it an exception? That is what we are discussing now.

    If it is a miracle, can it happen to you? It is not a miracle; it is not something given from above so that one can ask: How did this happen with this person and not with another—right?

M: What can we do?

K: I say you can do nothing—which does not mean doing nothing!

M: What are these two meanings of nothing?

K: I will tell you the two meanings of nothing: the one refers to desire to experience 'That', to recognize 'That' and yet to do nothing about 'That'. The other is to do nothing, in the other sense, it is to see or to be aware, not theoretically but actually, of the known.

M: You say, 'Do nothing, just observe.'

K: Put it that way if you want.

M: It brings down the enlightenment to action.

K: You must touch this thing, very very lightly. You must touch it very lightly—food, talk—and as the body and the senses become very light the days and nights move easily. You see there is a dying every minute. Have I answered, or very nearly answered, the question?

P: You have not answered specifically.

K: To put the whole thing differently: We will call 'That', for the moment, infinite energy and the other, energy created by strife and conflict—it is entirely different from 'That'. When there is no conflict at all the infinite energy is always renewing itself. The energy that peters out is what we know. What is the relationship of the energy that peters out to 'that'? There is none.

How Deep Can One Travel?

P: Sir, how deep can one travel?

K: Could we put the question this way? Most of our lives are very superficial and is it possible to live at great depth and also function superficially? Is it possible for the mind to dwell or live at great depth? I am not sure that we are all asking the same thing. We lead superficial lives and most of us are satisfied with that.

P: We are not satisfied. But we don't know how to go deep.

K: Most of us put up with it. Now, how is the mind to penetrate into great depth? Are we discussing depth in terms of measurement? Depth involves measurement. I want to be clear that we are not using the word in the sense of measurement or in the sense of time, but as something profound. These words have time significance, but we will wash away all the significance of time and measurement. We are asking whether the mind which generally lives superficially can penetrate to great depth? That is the question. I say it needs a build-up of energy, drive, and ask how is this energy to build up?

P: I know no other dimension. It needs a build-up of energy which drives through. How is the energy to be built up, or is it a wrong question?

K: Let us forget the word 'energy' for the time being. I lead a very superficial life and I see the beauty, intellectually or verbally, of a life, of a mind that has gone into itself very very deeply. Now, I say to myself I see the beauty of it, I see the quality of it, how is this to be done? Let us stick to that, instead of bringing in energy and all that. How is this to be done? Can thought penetrate it? Can thought become profound?

Please, sirs, do listen to this. I live a superficial life. I want to live a different kind of life, at great depth. I understand depth to mean not measurement or time to go down but depth as the bottomless; that which you cannot fathom, and I wannt to find it and live with it. Now, tell me what am I to do? I don't know. I am asking whether thought which is time, which is the past, whether thought can penetrate into this profundity?

Just listen to what I am saying. I see very clearly any measurable depth is still within a small measurement. I see the going down as involved in time, it may take years, and so I see intellectually, reasoning it out, I see depth means a timeless, measureless quality, an infinite without ever reaching the bottom. It is not a concept. It is not verbal to me. I have only verbalized it to you. Therefore, it becomes a concept to you.

M: Do you put the question to me or am I putting the question to myself?

K: I am putting the question to myself and therefore asking you to put the question to yourself. I see my life is a superficial life. That's obvious. So, I say to myself: Can thought penetrate this depth as thought is the only instrument I have?

Q: In that case, we cannot use the instrument.

R: How does one come upon this depth without using the instrument?

K: I live a very, very superficial life and I want to find out for myself if there is any depth which is not measurable and I see thought cannot reach it because thought is a measure, thought is time, thought is the response of the past; therefore thought cannot possibly touch it. Then, what will bring this about? If thought cannot touch it and that is the only instrument man has, then, what is he to do? Thought in its movement, in its function, has created this world which is superficial in which I live, of which I am. That is obvious. Now, is it possible for the mind, without the usage of thought, to touch something which is fathomless? Not just some moments in my sleep or when I am walking by myself, but to live there. My mind says the depth must be discovered, to let the

37

mind be of the quality of that—I must be aware of that strange fathomless depth of something which is unnamed.

P: Into what does one penetrate, delve?

K: I won't use those words.

P: No, sir. Thought is the instrument of measurement. There has to be freedom from the measurement-making machinery.

K: No, no. Be simple about this.

P: Can you delve into what is thought?

K: We have been into that. Thought is time, thought is measure, thought is the response of memory, thought is knowledge, experience, past, therefore the past is time. That thought must function always superficially. That is simple.

P: What you have said just now ends up in a big abstraction.

K: No.

P: It does, sir.

K: It is not an abstraction. It is a reality. But what is thought?

P: You said thought is time. You have abstracted that out of thought.

K: Thought cannot penetrate it. That is all. Leave it like that.

P: As it is the instrument that measures, can you penetrate this instrument?

K: No, I am concerned with depth, not with the machinery of measurement. The machinery of measurement is fairly obvious, I don't have to delve into all that.

P: If you say that, then I say into what dimension does one penetrate? If you won't have that and thought being the only instrument we know, into what dimension does one penetrate without thought?

K: There is no question of penetration.

38

P: Then what is it?

Q: We are still bound by the available machinery of construction we have, which is not in a position to reveal that fathomless state which we want to live in, because language is delicate. That instrument is too frail. We must have the language to deal with that dimension. We must have the tool to communicate.

P: What is the tool? Language is too frail. I cannot tell you about 'how' when I am that state.

K: Are we concerned with verbal communication or are we concerned with the touching of that depth?

Q: I know that sometimes I do touch. How can I tell you about that state?

P: You said that you don't use the existing instrument which you have, which is thought.

R: But I think Krishnaji has pointed out the difference: that it is not a question of occasionally feeling that, but how to be in it, to live in it.

K: As you eat, appetite comes. Leading a superficial life, as human beings do, I say to myself I would like to find that depth, where there is great width and beauty, something immense. Now, what am I to do? What is the other operation or the other movement that must take place when thought is not functioning? Can the mind remain without measure?

P: The question then is: Can that state come into being where there is no measure?

K: That is all. All your life you have known measure. Now, I am asking you: Can the mind be without measure?

P: If I were to ask you 'how', you would say 'no'. The only thing left then is to observe your mind measuring because there is no other way.

K: Have you done that? Have you observed, has the mind observed its movement and measurement?

P: Yes.

K: Comparing, measuring and ending. Then what?

P: Then there is stillness.

K: You say the movement of measurement has come to an end. Would that be right? Can you honestly, really say the movement with measurement has come to an end?

P: Just now it has come to an end.

K: That is not good enough. Good enough means that right through my life measurement has to come to an end.

P: How can I know it?

K: I am going to find out. I want to find out if my mind which has been conditioned in the movement of measurement—measurement equals comparison, imitation, conformity, an ideal, a resistance which safeguards it from non-measurement—can the mind say: 'Now I have understood the whole movement of measurement and I see where its legitimate place is and where it has no place at all'?

P: How is that understood by the mind in which there is no thought?

K: It perceives. I will show it to you. Thought has investigated and analysed it for the moment, thought has enquired, pushed, investigated, and it says it has seen the whole movement of measurement and that very perception of that movement is the ending of that movement. The very perception of it, that is, the seeing is the acting and ending. Seeing that this movement is time, is measure, seeing the whole map of it, the nature of it, the structure of it, that very perception acts in ending it. So, the seeing is the ending. There is no effort involved in it all. You say, 'I have seen this.' Have you?

Action in Attention

K: I wonder what we mean by action.

M: Action invariably means change.

K: I want to find out the meaning of the words 'to act', 'to do', not 'having done' or 'will do', either in the past or in the future. Acting is always in the active present, not as past action or future action, but action which is now.

P: Can there be action now?

K: I want to find out, Pupul, whether there is an action which is continuous and, therefore, always a movement without a causation. I am exploring, just move with me.

P: What do you mean by action?

K: Must action always have a cause, a motive, a direction?

P: Is it not a problem of the mind? Action is 'to do'. It is related to something. What is the movement of action?

K: The past, the present and the future. We know that. What do we mean by action? To do, the physical doing, the going from here to there, intellectually or emotionally working out a problem? So, action to us means 'operating on', 'operating through', or 'operating from'. I am just exploring. Is there an action without producing conflict—outside or inside? Is there an action which is whole, not fragmented? Is there an action which is a movement unrelated to environment, unrelated to me or to the community? Is there an action which is a movement out of time? All that to me is action. But to us action is in relationship to another. Action is related to the community we live in. Our action is dictated by the economic, climatic, personal, environmental condition. It is based on beliefs, ideals and so on. That is the action we know. Now, I want to find out if there is an action, which is not the result of environmental pressure.

M: Action is not a separate movement. To be here or *to be* is to act.

K: I want to see what is action. You are not helping me. What is action, moving from here to there, snatching a child from the road when a car is coming? Thinking about something and acting?

M: It is the motivation that matters.

K: Motivation is part of action. I want something and I get it. I don't like you and I act, or I like you and act. We know that. We are trying to find out what is action?

P: If it is obvious, then, what is the fact which propels that movement?

K: Pupulji, I think we have to eliminate causation in action. Is that possible?

P: We have started something which is a movement in a direction. In attention there is also movement. It is not that one goes to sleep with it. I am speaking to you now or Maurice is speaking to you and we are listening to you and there is no other movement within us. The question is: In this state, which has nothing except seeing you, what is it that motivates, moves?

K: I want to get at something much deeper. What is the action which is self-energizing? An action which is infinite movement with infinite energy? Am I making something clear? I think that is action. I am feeling my way into something. I feel all our actions are fragmented. All our actions are destructive: all our actions breed division and out of that division arises conflict. Our actions are always within the field of the known and, therefore, bound to time and therefore not free. That is so. Now I want to find out if there is any other action. We know action in the field of the known. We know technological action, the action of thought, the action of behaviour. Is there any other action?

42

P: How is this stream, the 'other action', contacted by or related to the brain cells? If it is not related to the brain cells and consciousness, then it would be synonymous with God.

K: I am asking what is action? Within the field of consciousness, we know action very well. It is all within the field of the known. I feel that such action must lead to various forms of frustration, sorrow, disintegration. Now, let us go slowly. I ask myself: Is there any other action which does not belong to this consciousness with its frustration, failures, sorrows, misery, confusion? Is there any action which is not of time? Is that a legitimate question? One has acted always within the field of the known. I want to find out if there is an action which is without friction. That is all. I know every action breeds some kind of friction. I want to find out an action which is non-contradictory, which does not bring conflict.

A: You would not be here if the motive was not there.

K: This does not mean that action is consistent, follows a set pattern. Following a pattern leads to a complete destruction of the brain. Such action is a mere mechanical repetition. I want to find out an action which is not repetitive, which is not conflicting, which is not imitative, conforming and therefore corrupt.

M: To live means to act on environment.

K: Therefore, I don't depend on environment. I want to live a life without conflict, which means life is action. And I see that life always has conflict in it. And I want to find a way of living which is action in which there is no conflict. Conflict means imitation, conformity and following a pattern in order not to have conflict, which is a mechanical way of living. Can we find a way of living in which there is not a breath of imitation, conformity, suppression? First of all, it is not a question of 'finding', let us remove the word 'finding'. It is a living now, today, in which there is no conflict.

M: Such action may be disastrous?

K: It won't be disastrous. My intelligence, looking at all the actions in the field of the known, observing them, paying attention to them, my intelligence asks this question. Intelligence is in operation now.

A: My intelligence tells me that I cannot hurt another without hurting myself much more. In the world, there is no such thing as doing evil to another without doing a greater evil to yourself.

K: The word 'intelligence' means not only to have a very alert mind, but to read between the lines. I read between the lines of the known activity. Having read that, my intelligence says that in the field of the known, action will be contradictory.

P: We appear to be totally blocked here. You say something and there is no way to find out, there is no way to talk about it.

K: I said I am going to investigate.

M: When intelligence searches for something, what happens?

P: What is the difference between the words 'investigate' and 'search'?

K: There is a great difference. Investigate means to 'trace out'. Search means 'seeking something to find'.

P: How will you investigate this?

M: In science, investigation means finding the unknown.

K: I take the word 'investigate', not what science means or what I mean. According to the dictionary, investigation means 'to trace out'. I see that any action with a motive must inevitably bring about a diversion, contradiction. I see that, not as an idea, but as a fact. So, I say, is there in my mind any contradiction when I am investigating it. I want to see what happens. I see, in paying attention, that an action based on a belief is contradictory. So, I say to myself: Is there a belief which is living, acting and therefore contradictory? If there is, I go after that belief and wipe it out.

P: Who is it who goes after that?

K: In that attention there is no going after, there is no wiping away. From that attention, observation, belief ends in me, not in

44

you. It ends. In that attention, I see that any form of conformity breeds fear, suppression, obedience. So, in that very attention, I wipe that away in me, and any action based on reward or punishment is out, finished. So, what has happened? I see that any action in relationship, based on an image, divides people. In paying attention to the known, all the factors of the known, their structure and their nature, end. And then attention becomes very important. Attention says: 'Is there any action which has none of these things?'

M: Would you say that attention itself has none of these things?

A: Would you say that attention itself is action?

K: That is it. Therefore, attention is perception in action and therefore in that there is no conflict. It is infinite. The action of a belief is wastage of energy. Action in attention is producing its own energy and it is endless. The brain has functioned always in the field of conflict, belief, imitation, conformity, obedience, suppression; it has always functioned that way and when the brain begins to know that, then attention begins to work. The brain cells themselves become attentive.

M: From what I have now understood, you seem to say that attention calls for energy and then energy directs.

K: Attention is action. We also said, consciousness is its content.

P: In a state of attention, do the brain cells themselves undergo change?

M: Biologically, every cell is individual, able to recharge energy and, therefore, to function. Every cell also functions because awareness is built into the cells.

K: I think so. I would like to start from a different point. The brain cells have gone through wastage of energy which is conflict, imitation, all the rest of it.. They are accustomed to that. The brain cells now have stopped that. They are out of that field, and the brain is no longer the residue of all that. It may function technologically and so on, but the brain that sees life is action and is without

45

conflict, is in a state of attention. When there is complete attention, right inside, not imposed, not directed, not willed, then the whole structure is alive; not in the usual sense, but in a different sense. I think there is a physical transformation. I think it is a direction of death and death is that. So, there is an action which is non-repetitive and therefore freedom from the known is attention in the unknown.

P: Freedom from the known is also within the brain cells. The brain cells are the known but the freedom from the known is also within the brain cells.

K: Therefore, there is a definite transformation coming into being.

M: The brain is clear of engrams; that is a physical transform-ation.

K: This logically is so in the sense that as long as the mind is functioning within the field of the known, it is functioning in a groove and the brain cells have been functioning in grooves. Now when those grooves are non-existent, the total brain acts, not in grooves, but in freedom, which is attention.

Silence and Disorder

P: Can we discuss what is silence? Does silence have many facets or forms? How is it reached? Does it imply only the absence of thought? Or is the silence which arises through various experiences and situations, different in nature, dimension and direction?

K: Where shall we start? Are you saying: Is there a right approach to silence and if there is, what is it? And are there different varieties of silence, which means different methods by which to arrive at silence? What is the nature of silence? Shall we go into it in that order? First, is there a right approach to silence and what do we mean by 'right'?

P: Is there only one approach? If all the silences are of the same nature, then there may be many approaches.

K: I am just asking: What do we mean by the right approach?

P: The only one as against the many.

K: Therefore, what is the one? What is the approach which is true, natural, reasonable, logical and beyond logic? Is that the question?

P: I would not put it that way. I would say that silence is when consciousness is not operating, when thought is not operating. Silence is generally defined as the absence of thought.

K: I can go blank without any thought, just repeat something and go blank. Is that silence?

S: How do you know what is true silence?

K: Let us begin by asking: Is there a right approach to silence and what is that right approach? Are there many varieties of silences and is silence the absence of thought? In that a great many things

47

are implied such as: I can go blank suddenly; I am thinking and I just stop and look at something and then go blank—day-dreaming. I would like to approach this question by asking: Is there a true approach to silence? You started with that question. I think we ought to take that first and go into other things afterwards.

S: You seem to be giving emphasis to the true approach rather than to the true nature of silence.

K: I think so, because there are people who have practised silence by controlling thought, mesmerizing themselves into silence, controlling their chattering mind to such an extent that the mind becomes absolutely dull, stupid and silent. So I want to start with the enquiry from the point of right approach; otherwise we will wander off. Is there a natural, healthy, logical, objective, balanced approach to silence? Could we proceed from that? What is the necessity for silence?

P: The need for silence is easy to understand. Even in ordinary living when a constantly chattering, constantly irritated mind comes to rest, there is a feeling of being refreshed. The mind is refreshed quite apart from anything else, so silence in itself is important.

B: And also, even in the ordinary sense there is no seeing of colour, there is no seeing of things unless there is a certain quality of silence.

S: Then there is the whole tradition that maintains that silence is important, is necessary and the various systems of pranayama, breath control, exist to ensure it. So there are many states of silence and you cannot distinguish between an unhealthy state and a healthy one.

K: Supposing you don't know anything of what other people have said and why you should be silent, would you ask the question?

P: Even at the level of the tranquillizer, we would ask the question.

K: So you ask the question in order to tranquillize the mind.

P: Yes.

48

K: Because the mind is chattering and that is wearisome and exhausting. So do you ask whether there is a way of tranquillizing the mind without drugs? We know the way of tranquillizing the mind with drugs, but is there another way which will naturally, healthily, sanely, logically bring about tranquillity in the mind? How would you approach this? Being weary, exhausted by the chattering of the mind, I ask myself, 'Can I, without the use of drugs, quieten the mind?'

S: There are many ways of doing it.

K: I don't know of any. You all say there are many ways. I say, how can the mind do this without effort? Because effort implies disturbance of the mind, it does not bring about tranquillity, it brings about exhaustion. And exhaustion is not tranquillity. Conflict will not bring about tranquillity, it will bring about exhaustion and that may be translated as silence by those who are completely tired out at the end of the day. I can go into my meditation room and be quiet. But is it possible to bring about tranquillity in the mind without conflict, without discipline, without distortion—all those are exhausting processes.

S: When pranayama is done there is no conflict, it does not exhaust you but there is silence. What is its nature?

K: There you are breathing, getting more oxygen into your system and the oxygen naturally helps you to be relaxed.

S: That is also a state of silence.

K: We will discuss the states of silence afterwards; I want to find out whether the mind can become tranquil without any kind of effort, breathing, enforcement, control, direction.

Par: The mind only asks the question whether it is possible to have tranquillity without conflict because it is agitated, disturbed.

K: I asked: Can there be silence without conflict, without direction, without enforcement of any kind? I can take a drug, a tranquillizer and make the mind very quiet. It is on the same level as pranayama; I control the mind and silence can be brought about.

49

It is on the same level as breathing, or drugs. I want to start from a point where the mind is agitated, chattering, exhausting itself by incessant friction of thought, and ask whether it is possible to be really quiet without any artificial means? To me that is a central issue. I would approach it that way if I went into this. I would discard artificial controls—drugs, watching the breath, watching light, mantras, bhajans—all these are artificial means and induce a particular kind of silence.

S: Are they external, motivated?

K: It is all part of it. I would consider all these means as artificial enforcements in order to induce silence. What happens when you look at a mountain? The greatness, the beauty, the grandeur of the mountains absorb you. That makes you silent. But that is still artificial. I would consider any form of inducement to bring about silence artificial.

S: Looking at a mountain is a non-dualistic experience. How can you then say that it is still not silence?

K: I would not call it silence because the thing is so great that for the time being its greatness knocks you out.

S: The absence of the 'me' is not at the conscious level, but it is there.

K: You see a marvellous picture, a marvellous sunset, an enormous chain of mountains and it is like a child being absorbed with a toy; that greatness knocks out the 'me' for the moment and the mind becomes silent. You can experiment with it.

S: But you say that is not silence.

K: I would not call that silence because the mountain, the beauty of something, takes over for the moment. The 'me' is pushed aside; and the moment that is gone, I am back to my chattering. At least I want to be clear that any artificial act with a motive, with a direction, seems to K a distortion which will not bring about the depth of silence. In this are included practices, discipline, control, identification with the greater and thereby making oneself quiet,

50

and so on. Then I ask myself: What is the necessity of silence? If there was no motive, would I ask that question?

Par: Are you describing your mind?

K: No, sir, I am not describing my mind. I said: Any inducement in any form, subtle or obvious, would not bring about the depth of great silence. I would consider it superficial; I may be wrong, we are enquiring.

Par: The state of your mind is already a silent mind.

K: May be, I don't know. So what is the natural, healthy approach to tranquillity?

R: But an approach is a motivation.

K: I would not use that word. What is the state of natural tranquillity? How does one come upon it naturally? If I want to listen to what you are saying, my mind must be quiet—that is a natural thing. If I want to see something clearly, the mind must not be chattering.

P: In that state lies all poise, all harmony.

K: I would say the basis for the depth of silence is poise, harmony between the mind, the body and the heart, great harmony, and the putting aside of any artificial methods, including control. I would say the real basis is harmony.

P: You have used another word: 'harmony'. How does this solve the problem? The only thing I know is conflict. I don't know silence.

K: Therefore, don't talk about silence. Deal with conflict, not with silence. If there is disharmony between the mind, the body, the heart, etc. deal with that, not with silence. If you deal with silence, being disharmonious, then it is artificial. This is so.

P: An agitated mind naturally seeks a state of non-agitation.

K: Be concerned with the agitated mind, not with silence. Deal with 'what is' and not with what might be.

R: Are you asking whether the agitated mind can deal with its own agitation?

K: That is a different question.

B: She is saying that the agitated mind naturally asks the question.

K: Yes, so be concerned, not with silence, but with why the mind is agitated.

P: It seeks the opposite state.

K: Then it is in conflict. The concept has its roots in its own opposite.

R: The concept itself is part of agitation.

K: I would say complete harmony is the foundation for the purity of silence.

S: How does one know of this complete harmony?

K: Let us go into that. We will later on come to the question of varieties of silences. So, what is harmony?

P: Does harmony arise when conflict ends?

K: I want to find out what is harmony between the mind, the body and the heart, a total sense of being whole without fragmentation, without the over development of the intellect, but with the intellect operating clearly, objectively, sanely; and the heart not operating with sentiment, emotionalism, outbreaks of hysteria, but with a quality of affection, care, love, compassion, vitality; and the body with its own intelligence, not interfered with by the intellect. The feeling that everything is operating, functioning beautifully like a marvellous machine is important. Is this possible?

Q: In that harmony is there a centre?

K: I don't know, we can find out. Can the mind, the brain function efficiently, without any friction, any distraction? Can the mind have the intelligence, the capacity to reason, to perceive, to be clear? When there is a centre it is obviously not possible, because the centre is translating everything according to its limitations. Am I reducing everybody to silence?

R: Why does this division arise between the mind and the body?

K: It arises through our education, where emphasis is laid on the cultivation of the intellect as memory and reason, as a function apart from living.

R: That is the over-emphasis on the mind. Even without education, there can be an over-emphasis on emotions.

K: Of course. Man worships the intellect much more than the emotions. Does he not? An emotion is translated into devotion, into sentimentality, into all kinds of extravagance.

Par: How does one differentiate between the accumulation of memory for technical or day-to-day purposes, and the accumulation of emotional memory?

K: That is very simple, sir. Why does the brain as the repository of memory, give such importance to knowledge—technological, psychological, and in relationship? Why have human beings given such extraordinary importance to knowledge? I have an office. I become an important bureaucrat, which means I have knowledge about performing certain functions and I become pompous, stupid, dull.

Par: Is it an innate desire?

K: It gives security—obviously. It gives you status. Human beings have worshipped knowledge—knowledge as identified with the intellect. The erudite person, the scholar, the philosopher, the inventor, the scientist, are all concerned with knowledge and they have created marvellous things in the world, like going to the moon, making new kinds of submarines and so on. They have invented the most extraordinary things and the admiration, the marvel at that knowledge is overwhelming and we accept it. So we have developed an inordinate admiration, almost verging on worship, of the intellect. This applies to all the sacred books and their interpretations. Correct me, if I am wrong. In contrast to that, there is a reaction to be emotional, to have feeling, to love, to have devotion, sentimentality, extravagance in expression, and the body gets neglected. You see this and therefore you practise yoga. This division between the body, the mind and the heart takes place unnaturally. Now we have to bring about a natural harmony where the intellect functions like a marvellous watch, where the emotions and affections, care, love and compassion are healthily functioning and the body, which has been so despoilt, which has been so misused, comes into its own. Now how do you do that?

GM: I adore knowledge because I need it.

K: Of course, I need it. It is very clear, sir, I need knowledge to talk to you in English. To ride a bicycle, to drive an engine, needs knowledge.

Q: I have to solve the problem of disease. I need knowledge to deal with it. That is still within the field of knowledge.

K: Knowledge is misused by the centre as the 'me' which has got knowledge. Therefore I feel superior to the man who has less knowledge. I use knowledge to provide a status for myself; I am more important than the man who has no knowledge.

S: If I may say so, we started the discussion with silence and the various ways in which we arrive at silence. You pointed out that unless there is harmony, we cannot have a basis for questioning or for asking what silence is.

D: Do we not make a distinction between knowledge and the discovery of the new?

K: Of course, sir. When knowledge interferes there is no discovery of the new. There must be an interval between knowledge and the new; otherwise you are just carrying on the new like the old. R asked: 'Why is there division between the mind, the heart and the body.' We see that. How is this division to come to an end naturally? How do you do it—through enforcement, through the ideals we have of harmony?

54

Sir, one is aware of this division—isn't one—between the intellect, the emotions and the body. There is this gap between all of them. How is the mind to remove this gap and be whole? What do the traditionalists say?

M: Effort, clench your teeth.

P: We are getting bogged down. We started with silence. We don't touch silence; then you used the word 'harmony' and we can't touch harmony.

K: Then what will you do? We will return to silence.

P: We come back to only one thing, which is, we know only disharmony.

K: Therefore let us deal with disharmony and not with silence and when there is the understanding of disharmony, from that may flow silence.

S: Also there is the question: How does one know that one has ended disharmony totally?

M: There is a Latin saying, 'I know what is right, but I don't follow it.'

K: Don't bring in anything from the Latin. Face the thing as it is. Pupul says we started out with silence and we said it is no good discussing silence until you find out if there is a natural way of coming to it. The artificial way is not the way. The natural way is to find out if there is harmony, but we don't know anything about harmony because we are in a state of disorder. So let us deal with disorder, not with harmony, not with silence.

M: I observe my disorder and the disorder goes on looking at me.

K: Therefore there is a duality, a division, a contradiction in your observation, as the observer and the observed. We can play with this endlessly. Please follow what we have so far discussed. We started out with asking: What is the nature of silence, are there different varieties of silence, are there different approaches to silence? Pupul also asked: 'What is the right way to silence?' We

55

said, perhaps there may be a 'right' way, but that any artificial means to bring about silence is not silence; we made that very clear. Don't let us go back. If there is no artificial way, is it possible to come upon silence naturally, without effort, without inducement, without direction, without artificial means? In examining this we came to harmony. To that Pupul says: 'We don't know what harmony is, but what we do know is disorder.' So let us put aside everything else and consider disorder, not what silence is. A mind that is in disorder enquires after silence. Silence then becomes a means of bringing about order or escape from disorder. Silence then is imposed on disorder. So we stop all that and ask: Why is there disorder? Is it possible to end disorder?

P: There is disorder when thought arises and I want silence.

K: No, you are looking for a cause, you want to find out what is the cause of disorder.

P: I don't.

K: Then?

P: I observe the nature of disorder. I don't look for the cause. I don't know.

K: One observes disorder in oneself.

P: I see that it is manifested as thought.

K: I don't know. I would like to go into it very carefully because it is rather interesting. Why do I call what I observe disorder?

S: Disturbance is disorder.

K: I just want to find out. Why do I call it disorder? Which means I already have an inkling of what order is. So I am comparing what I have experienced or known as order and thereby ask what is disorder. I don't do that. I say, don't compare, just see what disorder is. Can the mind know disorder without comparing it with order? So, can my mind cease comparing? Comparison may be disorder. Comparison itself may be the cause of disorder. Measurement may be disorder, and as long as I am comparing,

56

there must be disorder. I am comparing my disorder at present with a whiff of order which I have smelt and I call it disorder. So I see it is comparison which is really important, not disorder. As long as my mind is comparing, measuring, there must be disorder.

R: Without comparing I look at myself and I see there is disorder because every part of me is pulling in a different direction.

K: I have never felt that I am in disorder, except rarely, occasionally. I say to myself: Why are all these people talking about disorder?

D: Do they really know disorder or do they only know it through comparison?

P: You bring in words which I find very difficult to understand. There is no conscious comparison by the mind which says, 'This is disorder and I want to end it.' I know disorder.

A: A sense of uneasiness.

P: I see a sense of confusion, one thought against another thought. You will say the word 'confusion' is again comparison. I know confusion.

K: You only know contradiction, which is confusion. Stick to that. You say your mind is in a state of confusion because it is contradicting itself all the time. Proceed from that.

B: There is a real difficulty here. You talked about silence, then about harmony, then about disorder. Why do we speak of disorder? We function partly in order also.

P: I am sorry, I don't know either harmony or silence. I say I observe my mind, I see disorder.

K: Then what? From there move.

P: Then I am bound to ask: Is it the nature of the mind?

K: Ask.

P: I ask, and there must be a way out of this.

57

K: Then what?

P: Then I observe myself asking that question.

K: Yes.

P: For the time being the activity of the mind comes to an end.

M: What is the fallacy in this?

K: There is no fallacy in this. I am coming to that.

P: Look, sir, we need not have gone through this. But I thought it was better to go step by step. There is an ending here. May be to someone else there may not be an ending, but for me there is. What is the nature of this? I now come back to my first question: Is the undercurrent in that ending still operating? When we talk of different qualities and natures and dimensions of silence it means just this. The traditional outlook is that the gap between two thoughts is silence.

K: That is not silence. Silence between two notes is not silence. Listen to that noise outside. Absence of noise is not silence. It is only an absence of noise.

P: There is an ending of the perception of oneself in a state of disturbance.

K: Pupul, you have not been clear. When you say 'disorder' I am not at all sure that you know what disorder is. You call it disorder. I over-eat, that is disorder. I over-indulge in emotional nonsense, that is disorder.

P: I catch myself talking very loudly and that is disorder.

K: So what is disorder? How do you know it is disorder? Listen, I over-eat; I have tummy-ache. I don't call it disorder. I say, 'I over-ate, I must not eat so much.'

P: We moved from silence to harmony and we found that it is impossible to go into the nature of harmony without going into disorder.

K: That is all. Keep to those three points.

58

P: Why do you call it disorder?

R: It is not necessarily a recognition of disorder, because when there is a conflict between the body, the mind . . .

K: You associate conflict with disorder.

R: No, the conflict makes one weary, as you say, and one instinctively feels that there is something wrong with it.

K: So what you are saying is, if I understand it rightly, conflict indicates disorder.

R: Even when you don't name it.

K: Conflict *is* disorder. You translate it as disorder. Don't move around in circles.

P: I say you must be free of conflict.

M: Of disorder.

K: Which is the same thing. Silence, harmony, conflict. That is all—not disorder.

P: Forgive me for saying it but you can take the word 'conflict' and go through the same gymnastics with it as you did with the word 'disorder'. But what do I do about conflict?

K: That is all we are concerned with: silence, harmony, conflict. How am I to deal with conflict non-artificially? You know nothing. You are listening for the first time. You have to go into it with me. Don't say 'How do I look at it for the first time?' Somebody comes and says: 'Look at this marvellous machinery'. You look.

S: This much I can see clearly. I cannot think of silence or harmony when I am in conflict.

K: Is the mind capable of freeing itself from every kind of conflict? That is the only thing you can ask. What is wrong with that question?

R: It is the mind again which is asking the question.

S: It is a legitimate question.

P: Can the mind be free of disharmony? I don't see the difference between the two.

K: We have reduced it to conflict. Now stick to it and see if the mind can be free of it. How can the mind, knowing what conflict is and what it does, end conflict? That is surely a legitimate question.

M: Because you assume that the mind can do it.

K: I don't know.

Q: If we look into this question of conflict, look into various aspects of it, we see there is no conflict without comparison.

K: Conflict is contradiction, comparison, imitation, conformity, suppression. Put all that into one word and accept the meaning of the word as we defined it, and ask whether the mind can be free of conflict.

S: Of course it can be free of conflict, but the question arises: What is the nature of that freedom from conflict?

K: How do you know before you can be free?

S: There is a knowing of the state of conflict for the time being.

K: Is there a complete ending of conflict?

S: That's why I asked the question: Is there a total ending of conflict?

M: I say there is no ending of conflict in the universe as we live in it from day to day.

K: Don't include the universe. In the universe everything is moving in order. Let us stick to our minds which seem to be endlessly in conflict. Now, how is the mind to end conflict naturally, because every other system is a compulsive, a directional method, a method of control and all that is out. How can the mind free itself from conflict? I ask: Where are you at the end of it? I say, the mind can be completely, utterly without conflict.

S: For ever?

K: Don't use the words 'for ever' because you are then introducing a word of time and time is a matter of conflict.

P: I want to ask you a question. Can the mind be totally in conflict?

K: What are you trying to say? I don't quite understand.

P: You see, I feel myself totally helpless in this situation. The fact is there is conflict and the operation of the self on it leads to further conflict. Seeing the nature of that, can the mind see that it is totally in conflict?

K: Can the mind be aware of a state in which there is no conflict? Is that what you are trying to say? Or can the mind only know conflict? Right? Is your mind totally aware of conflict, or is it just a word? Or is there a part of the mind which says 'I am aware that I am totally in conflict and there is a part of me watching conflict.' Or is there a part of the mind wishing to be free of conflict, which means, is there a fragment which says 'I am not in conflict' and which separates itself from the totality of conflict? If there is a separate fragment, then that fragment says: 'I must do, I must suppress, I must go beyond.' So this is a legitimate question. Is your mind totally aware that there is nothing but conflict or is there a fragment which skips away and says, 'I am aware that I am in conflict but I am not in total conflict.' So, is conflict a fragment or is it total? I will keep to the same word, not to be substituted by a different word, for the time being. Is there total darkness or a slight light somewhere?

R: If that light were not there, could there be awareness?

K: I don't know anything about it. Don't ask me that question. When there is a fragmentation of the mind, that very fragmentation is conflict. Is the mind ever aware that it is in total conflict? Pupul says 'yes'.

P: You have moved away.

K: I have not.

P: I don't know anything about total conflict.

K: Therefore you know only partial conflict.

P: No, sir, whether partial or not, we know the fact that there is conflict and I ask: Can there be a refusal to move away?

K: I have not moved away from silence, harmony or conflict.

P: Where is totality in this?

K: I think this is an important question.

R: Sir, the very awareness of the mind indicates that there is a fragment.

K: That is all. Therefore you say: Partially I am in conflict. Therefore you are never *with* conflict.

P: No, sir.

SWS: Total conflict cannot know itself unless there is something else.

K: We are going to go into that.

P: I am not making myself clear. The state of conflict does not have a wide, broad spectrum. When you say 'total', it fills the mind.

K: When the whole room is full of furniture—I am just taking that as an example—there is no space to move. I would consider that to be utter confusion. Is my mind so totally full of confusion that it has no movement away from this? Is it so completely full of confusion, of conflict, as full as this room is of furniture? Then what takes place? That is what I want to get at. We are not discussing the partial this and the partial that. When the steam is at full pressure it must explode, it must do something. I don't think we look at conflict totally. Could I use the word 'sorrow'? There is no moving away from sorrow. When you move away from sorrow, then it is just an escape. Is there such a thing as being full of sorrow? Is there such a thing as being completely happy? When you are aware that you are completely happy, you are no longer happy. In the same way, when you are completely full of this thing called confusion, sorrow, conflict, it is no longer there. It is only there when there is division. That is all.

R: No, sir, then it seems to be a hopeless problem.

K: That is why one has to remain with the truth of the thing, not with the confusion of it. There is the truth of the thing when the mind is complete with something; then it cannot create conflict. If I love you and there is attachment in it, that is a contradiction, therefore there is no love. So I say, remain with the fact of that thing. Is the mind totally full of this sorrow, this confusion, this conflict? I won't move away till that is so.

M: There is one peculiarity about your approach. When you draw a picture there is always a clear black outline. The colours don't merge. In reality there are no outlines, there are only colours merging with each other.

K: This to me is very clear. If the heart is full of love and there is no part of envy in it, the problem is finished. It is only when there is a part that is jealous, then the whole problem arises.

P: But when it is full of envy?

K: Then remain with that envy fully—*be* envious, feel it!

P: Then I know its total nature.

K: It is a tremendous thing. But you say, 'I am envious and I must not be envious.' Somewhere in a dark corner there lies the educational restraint; then something goes wrong. But can I be envious and not move from that? Moving away is rationalizing, suppressing, all that. Just remain with that feeling. When there is sorrow, be completely with it. This is merciless. All the rest is playing tricks. When you are *with* something, action has taken place. You don't have to do anything.

Factors of Deterioration

P: Could we discuss the problems of deterioration and death? Why is it that the mechanism of the mind has an inbuilt tendency to deteriorate, an ebbing away of energy?

K: Why does the body, the mind deteriorate?

P: With age, with time, the body deteriorates; but why does the mind deteriorate? At the end of life, there is the death of the body and the death of the mind. But the death of the mind can take place even when the body is alive. If, as you say, the brain cells contain consciousness, then, with the deterioration of the cells of the human body, is it not inevitable that the cells of the human mind, the brain, will also deteriorate?

K: Are we talking about the deterioration of the whole structure of the mind and the brain with age, with time? The biologists have given the answer. What do they say?

M: The cells of the brain and the body deteriorate because there is no process of elimination. They are not made for perpetual functioning. They do not completely eliminate the products of their own metabolism. If they were given a chance to wash themselves out completely, they could live for ever.

K: The question is: Why does the brain, which has been active during a certain period of time, deteriorate? And the biological answer to that is, given sufficient cleansing power, it can go on living for ever. What is the cleansing element?

M: Adequate elimination.

K: It is much deeper than that, surely.

M: Adequate elimination is the outer expression of the cleansing process.

64

P: That's not adequate. If that were so, the human body, if adequately cleansed, would not deteriorate. But death is inevitable. Is the mind different from the brain cells?

K: Is it a deterioration of energy or a deterioration of the brain cells in their capacity to produce energy? Let us first put the question clearly.

B: When we say that the brain deteriorates, the assumption is that the brain is very alive at some stage, but one of the problems of existence is the mediocrity of the mind.

K: The question is: Why does the brain not keep its quality of sharpness, clarity, deep energy? As it gets older, it seems to deteriorate. This happens even at the age of twenty. It is already held in a groove and gradually peters out. I want to find out if it is a matter of age. You can see that certain minds, even though they are quite young, have already lost this quality of swiftness. They are already caught in a groove and the deteriorating factor has already begun.

S: Is it that we are born with a certain conditioning? Is that the determining factor?

K: Is it a mattter of conditioning and the breaking through of that conditioning which frees energy and therefore enables the mind to go on indefinitely; or has the deterioration to do with a mind that functions in decisions?

S: What do you mean by functioning in decisions?

K: That which operates through choice and will. One decides the course of action one is going to take, and that decision is based not on clarity, not on the observation of the total field, but according to satisfaction and enjoyment, which are fragments of that field. And one continues to live in that fragmentation. That is one of the factors of deterioration. My choice to be a scientist may be based on environmental influence, family influence, or my own desire to achieve success in a certain direction. These many considerations being about the choice of a particular profession, and that decision, that choice and the action from that choice, is one of the factors

65

of deterioration. I disregard the rest of the field and only follow a particular narrow corner of that field. The brain cells do not function totally but only in one direction. See, this is rather interesting. Don't accept this. We are examining it.

P: Are you saying that the brain functions not fully, but only in one direction.

K: The whole brain is not active, and I think that is the factor of deterioration. You asked what are the factors of deterioration, not whether the mind is capable of seeing the total or not. I have observed for these many years that a mind that has followed a certain course of action disregarding the totality of action, deteriorates.

P: Let us explore that. The brain cells themselves have an inbuilt sense of time, sense of memory, instinct. They operate as reflexes. The very nature of operating in reflexes limits the brain from functioning totally. And we know no other way.

K: We are trying to find out what are the factors of deterioration. When we see what the factors are, perhaps we may get to the other, see the total.

P: One can think of twenty factors of conflict, for instance.

K: Let us not take too many. A pursuit, based on choice, which has the motive of satisfaction of fulfilment or the desire to achieve, that action must create conflict. So, conflict is one of the factors of deterioration. Perhaps that is the major factor of deterioration. I decide to become a politician. I decide to become a religious man. I decide to become an artist, a sanyasi; that decision is made by a conditioning brought about by a culture which is in its very nature fragmentary. That is, I decide to be a bachelor because from what I have seen, from what I have heard, I think that to attain God, Truth, Enlightenment, I must remain celibate. I disregard the whole structure of human existence, the biological, the sociological, and all the rest of it. That decision obviously brings about a conflict in me, a sexual conflict, a conflict in keeping away from people, and so on. That is one of the factors of the deterioration of the brain. I am only using one part of it. The very factor of dividing one sector of my life from the rest is a factor of deterioration. So, choice and will are factors of deterioration.

P: And yet they are the two instruments of action we have.

K: That's right. Let us look at it. All our life is based on these two factors: discrimination or choice and the action of will in the pursuit of satisfaction.

S: Why discrimination?

K: Discrimination is choice. I discriminate between this and that. We are trying to see what is the factor of deterioration, the root factor of deterioration. We may come upon something different also. I see choice and will in action are the factors of deterioration, and if you see that, then the question is, Is there an action which does not have in it these two elements, thèse two principles?

P: Let us take the other factors because there are many other factors; there is the inherited, there is also shock, for instance.

K: If I have inherited a dull, stupid mind, I am finished. I can go to various temples and churches but my brain cells themselves have been affected.

P: Then there is shock.

K: Which is what?

P: The action of life itself.

K: Why should life itself produce a shock?

P: It happens.

K: Why? My son dies, my brother dies. It produced a shock because I never realized that my son would die. I suddenly realize he is dead, it is neurological shock. Are you using the word 'shock' psychologically or physically?

P: It is a physical shock, it is neurological shock, the coming into actual contact with the validity of something which ends.

K: All right. Let us take shock—physical, psychological, emotional shock of suddenly losing something, losing somebody, the shock of being alone, the shock of something that has suddenly come to an end. The brain cells receive this shock. Now what will you do about it? Is that shock a factor of deterioration?

S: No, the way we respond to the shock is the factor.

P: Can one respond with a total quiet? The mind has registered something which it is unable to understand. There are depths beyond which it cannot respond. We are talking of shock and of new responses. To what depth has one penetrated?

K: Wait Pupulji, just go slowly. My son is dead, my brother is dead. It is a tremendous shock because we have lived together, played together. That shock has paralysed the mind, and the shock does paralyse it for the time being. How the mind comes out of it is the important factor. Does it come out with a hurt, with all the implications of hurt or does it come out without a single hurt?

S: I may not know. Consciously I may say I have worked it out. How do I know that there is not a trace of hurt?

D: Sir, Could it be that in the case of shock, there is a death, there is an ending completely of the pattern of mind and the very seeing of that is the ending of it?

K: That is all implied. When my brother dies or my son dies, my whole life changes. The change is the shock. I have to leave this house, I have to earn a different kind of livelihood, I have to do a dozen things. All that is implied in the word 'shock'. Now, I am asking whether that shock has left a mark or hurt, or not. If it has not left a single mark, a single hurt, a single scratch or a shadow of sorrow, then the mind comes out of it totally refreshed, totally new. But if it has been hurt, brutalized, then that is a factor of deterioration. Now, how does the mind consciously know that it is not hurt deeply, profoundly?

P: If it is hurt deeply, profoundly, does it mean that there is no hope and it is all over? Or is there a way of wiping away?

68

K: We are going to go into that, Pupulji. The shock is natural because I have suddenly been thrown out on the street, metaphorically speaking. Neurologically, psychologically, inwardly, outwardly, the whole thing has changed. How does the mind come out of this? That is the question. Does it come out with hurt or does it come out totally purged of all hurt? Are the hurts superficial, or so profound that the conscious mind cannot possibly know them at a given moment and, therefore, they will keep on repeating, repeating? All that is wastage of energy. How does the mind find out whether it is deeply hurt?

P: The superficial hurts one can dismiss, deal with, but the deep hurts . . .

K: How will you deal with them?

P: There is brutality, death, there is violence.

K: Don't bring in violence. How does the mind come upon the deep hurts? What is a hurt?

P: Deep pain.

K: Is there a deep hurt?

P: Yes.

K: What do you mean by deep hurt?

P: The really deep hurts are because of a crisis, the very nature of your being is on the edge of sorrow.

K: My brother dies, my son dies; husband, wife, whatever. It is a shock. The shock is a kind of hurt. I am asking is the hurt very deep and what do I mean by 'very deep'?

P: The depths of the unconscious are thrown up.

K: What is being thrown up?

P: Pain.

K: Pain, of which you have not been aware and shock reveals the pain. Now, was the pain there or the cause of pain there?

69

P: The cause of pain was there. The cause of pain was there of which I was not conscious. The shock comes and makes me aware of that pain.

M: What do you mean by saying shock creates pain?

K: Pain was there. It is one of the factors. My brother is dead, that is absolutely final. I cannot bring him back. The world faces this problem, not you and I alone, everybody faces this problem. There is a shock. That shock is a deep hurt. Was the cause of the hurt there before and the shock has only revealed it? Was the hurt there because I never faced it? I have never faced loneliness. I have never faced the sense of loneliness which is one of the factors of hurt.

Now, can I, before the shock comes, look at loneliness? Can I, before the shock comes, know what it is to be alone? Before the shock comes, can I go into this question of reliance, dependency, which are all factors of hurt, the causes of hurt, so that when the shock comes, they are all brought out. Now, when the shock comes, what happens? I have no hurt. This is right.

M: What makes you prepare yourself?

K: I don't prepare. I watch life. I watch what are the implications of attachment or indifference or the cultivation of independence because I must not depend. Dependence causes pain, but to cultivate independence may also bring pain. So, I watch myself, I watch and see that dependence of any kind must inevitably bring about deep hurt. So, when the shock comes, the cause of hurt is not. A totally different thing takes place.

S: It can happen that in order to prevent suffering, we do all that you have described.

P: Sir, all these things one has done. One has observed, one has gone into the problems of attachment.

K: Would you say shock is 'suffering'?

P: Shock seems to touch the depths of my being which I have never been able to touch before, to which I have had no access.

K: What do you mean by that? If you have gone through loneliness, attachment, fear, not seeking independence or detachment as an opposite to attachment, then what takes place? When shock comes, the shock of death, what takes place? Are you hurt?

P: That's a word I would like to enlarge upon. It seems to bring out all the pains I have had.

K: Which means what? You have not resolved the pain—not resolved the pain of loneliness. I am taking that as an example.

P: What I want to ask is: Is there a resolution of the pain of attachment or is it a complete comprehension of whatever is, an awakening to the total process of pain?

K: No. Look, suffering is pain. We use that suffering to cover loneliness, attachment, dependence, conflict. We use the whole field of man's escape from suffering and the cause of suffering. We use the word 'suffering' to include all that. Or, would you like to use the term 'the totality of pain'? The hidden and the observable totality of suffering—the pain of a villager, the pain and sorrow of a woman who has lost her husband, the sorrow of a man, ignorant, unlettered, always in poverty; and the sorrow of man, the pain of man who is ambitious, frustrated—all that is suffering and the shock brings all that pain, not only yours, to the surface. Agreed? What takes place? I don't know how to deal with it. I cry, I pray and go to the temple. This is what takes place. I hope to meet my brother or son in the astral plane. I do everything, trying to get out of this torture of pain. Why should the shock reveal all this?

P: The roots of pain have never been revealed.

K: Seeing that beggar on the road, leprous, or the villager endlessly working in sorrow, why has that not touched the human mind? Why should shock touch it?

P: Is there a why?

K: Why does that beggar not shock me personally and the whole of society? Why does it not move me?

71

D: The shock attacks the whole structure of pain and makes the structure of pain act.

K: I am asking you a simple question. You see the beggar on the road. Why is that not a shock to you? Why do you not cry? Why do I cry only when my son dies? I saw a monk in Rome. I cried to see the pain of someone tied to a post called religion. We don't cry there but we cry here. Why? There is a 'why', obviously. There is a 'why' because we are insensitive.

B: The mind is asleep. The shock wakes it up.

K: That's it. The shock wakes it up and we are awakened to pain, which is our pain: we were not awakened to pain before. This is not a theory.

P: No, sir, when you make a statement like that, I am awakened to pain and it is not a question of my pain . . .

K: It is pain. Now, what do you do with pain? Pain is suffering. What takes place?

P: It is like a storm. If one is in the middle of a storm, you don't ask 'why'. In it is every pain.

K: I said that it is not your pain; it is pain. I felt pain when I saw that beggar. When I saw that monk, I cried. When I saw that villager, I was tortured. When I saw the rich man, I said, 'My God, look.' Society, culture, religion, the whole life of man is also the pain of my losing my brother. So it is pain. What do I do with pain? Is it deep or superficial? You say it is very deep.

A: It is very deep.

K: What do you mean by 'deep'?

P: What I mean by 'deep' is that it goes through every part of my being. It is not sectional; it is not operating only in one part of my life.

K: You say 'It is very deep'. Don't call it deep. It has no measurement. It is not deep or shallow. Pain is pain. Then what? You remain in it, bear this hurt?

B: We cannot escape from it or substitute it.

K: So, what shall I do with the pain? Ignore it? We are going to find out. Do I go to the analyst to get rid of the pain, or do I read a book or go to Tirupati or to Mars to get rid of the pain? How shall I get rid of it? What shall I do with it?

P: I am in the position of standing still.

K: You are in pain. You are that pain. Hold it. You are there. You hold it. It is your baby, and then what? Let us find out. I am that pain—the pain of the villager, the pain of the beggar, the pain of that man who is rich who goes through agonies, the monk and all the rest of it. I am that pain. What shall I do?

B: Is there not a transformation of this pain into wakefulness?

K: That is what I want to find out.

S: At the moment of death, everything is thwarted.

K: At the moment of death, a few days after, my whole nervous, biological, psychological system is paralysed. I am not talking about that moment. Don't go back to it again. Now it has passed. It is a year old. I am left with this pain. What shall I do?

B: When there is an unintelligent operation of this brain, suffering does wake it up. Apparently, it is a very unintelligent operation.

K: A mother loses her son in Vietnam and yet mothers don't seem to learn that their sons might be killed through nationalism, through concepts and formulas. They don't realize it. That's pain. I realize that for them. I suffer. We suffer. There is suffering. What shall I do?

Rad: I will see what it is.

K: I see what it is. That beggar can never become a minister and that monk is tortured by his own vows, by his own ideas of God. I see all that. I see it so clearly. I don't have to examine it any more. What shall I do with it?

M: The understanding by which the beggar's pain and another's pain becomes your own pain is unknown to us. Not everybody can see the beggar's pain as his own pain.

K: I have that pain, what shall I do? I am not concerned whether everybody sees it or not. Many people do not see things. What shall I do? My son is dead.

P: You are in the middle of it. I am talking of being held by it and of being in it.

K: You heard that beggar singing last night. It was a terrible thing. The fact is there—the pain, the suffering. What will you do?

M: You act, try to change the condition of the beggar.

K: That is your fixed idea. You want to do it your way and somebody else wants to do it another way but I am talking about pain. We asked what are the factors of deterioration of the brain cells and the mind. We said one of the major factors is conflict. Another factor is hurt, pain. And what are the factors?—fear, conflict, suffering, and the pursuit of pleasure, call it God, social service, work for the country. So, these are the factors of deterioration. Who is to act? What am I to do? Unless the mind solves this, its action will produce more suffering, more pain.

P: The deterioration will be accelerated.

K: That's an obvious fact. We have come to the point of pain, hurt, suffering and the factor of fear, and the pursuit of pleasure, as a few factors that bring about deterioration. What shall I do? What shall the mind do?

SWS: By asking this, the mind tries to become something other than what it is.

K: If it is in pain, how can it act?

S: How can it become something else? Becoming is another factor of deterioration. Becoming is a factor because in it, there is conflict. I want to be something; therefore, becoming is the avoidance of pain, therefore conflict. So, what shall I do? I have tried village

74

work, I have tried social work, cinemas, sex, and yet pain remains. What shall I do?

Q: There must be some way to let the pain go.

K: Why should it go? All you are concerned with is to make it go. Why should it go? There is no way out, is that it?

SWS: You have to live with it.

K: How do you live with something which is pain, which is sorrow? How do you live with it?

Rad: When I stop doing anything about it.

K: Are you doing it or are you just saying it as a theory? What is the mind to do with this tremendous hurt which causes pain, suffering, this everlasting battle that brings about the deterioration of the brain cells?

B: One should try to watch it.

K: Watch what, sir? Is my suffering, is my pain different from the watcher? Is it? Is the pain different from the watcher? So, what takes place? The observer says, 'I must get rid of pain'. But it is still there at the end of the journey. Now, what takes place when the observer is the observed?

M: We started with what is the factor of deterioration. We have come to the conclusion that pain is the factor of deterioration. If we don't want deterioration, we must not suffer pain. Therefore, doing away with pain is important and we cannot say: 'I am pain,' 'I have to live with pain'. This is endless. We must cease to suffer. Now, what is the secret of it? You tell us.

K: Secret of what? You introduce words which I never used. I am using words according to the dictionary. I don't want to be a blank wall which does not feel.

M: Immunity does not mean insensitivity.

K: We all want to get rid of pain. It would be idiotic to say: 'I must endure pain', and that is what most people do, and because they

75

endure pain, they take neurotic action like going off to temples and so on. So, it is absurd to say that we must endure pain. On the contrary, knowing that pain is one of the major factors of deterioration, how does it come to an end? Sir, at the end of pain, the mind becomes extraordinarily passionate; it is not just a dull, painless mind. You want the secret of it?

M: Do you know the secret?

K: I will tell you. Do you want it? Let us approach it in a different way. Is it possible for a mind never to be hurt? Education hurts us, the family hurts us, society hurts us. I am asking: 'Can the mind, living in a world in which there is hurt, never be hurt?' You call me a fool. You call me a great man. You call me enlightened or wise or a stupid old man. Call me anything; can I never be hurt? It is the same problem put differently.

S: There is a slight difference. There the problem was one of being hurt and how to solve it. Here the question is: Is there a possibility of never being hurt?

K: I am showing it to you. That is the secret. What will you do with all the hurts that human beings have accumulated? If you don't solve this problem, do what you will, it will lead to more sorrow. Let us proceed. We just now asked what takes place when the observer is the observed.

SWS: There should be an observation without the centre.

K: Observation without the centre means there is only that thing which you call pain. There is no entity that says I must go beyond the pain. When there is no observer, is there pain? It is the observer that gets hurt. It is the centre that gets flattered. It is the centre that says it is shocked. It is the centre that says 'I know pain'. Now, can you observe this thing called pain without the centre, without the observer? It is not a vacuum. What takes place?

M: The pain changes the feeling.

K: What do you mean by saying that the pain changes the feeling? Sir, this is a difficult thing because we are always looking at pain

76

from the centre as the observer who says: 'I must do something.' So, action is based on the centre doing something about pain, but when the centre is pain, what do you do? What is there to be done?

What is compassion? The word 'compassion' means passion and how does that come? By chasing around activity? How does it come? When suffering is not, the 'other' is. Does this mean anything to you? How can a mind that suffers know compassion?

M: The knowledge that there is pain is compassion.

K: Forgive me. I never said become compassionate. We are seeing the fact, the 'what is', which is suffering. That is an absolute fact. I suffer and the mind is doing everything it can to run away from it. When it does not run away, then it observes. Then the observer, if it observes very very closely, is the observed, and that very pain is transformed into passion, which is compassion. The words are not the reality. So, don't escape from suffering, which does not mean you become morbid. Live with it. You live with pleasure, don't you? Why don't you live with suffering completely? Can you live with it in the sense of not escaping from it? What takes place? Watch. The mind is very clear, very sharp. It is faced with the fact. The very suffering transformed into passion is something enormous. From that arises a mind that can never be hurt. Full stop. That's the secret.

Energy and the Cultivation of the Field

P: Could we discuss one of the chief blockages to understanding, that is, the factor of self-centred activity?

K: When you talk about self-centredness, a centre implies a periphery. Can we say, where there is a centre there is a boundary, a limitation and all action must be within the circle of centre and periphery? That is self-centred activity.

P: What are the boundaries of the self?

K: It can be limitless or within the limits, but there is always a boundary.

D: Limitless?

K: You can push it as far as you like. As long as there is a centre, there is a periphery, a boundary, but that boundary can be stretched.

P: Does that mean, sir, there is no limit to this stretching?

K: Let us go slowly. When we talk about self-centred activity, that is what is implied—a centre and a periphery, a limitation and within that circle all action takes place: to think about oneself, to progress towards something is still from the centre to a periphery. Where there is a centre, there is a boundary, and that centre may expand itself, but it is still within that boundary, and therefore within that circle all action takes place. From the centre you can stretch as far as you like, through social service, democratic or electorate dictatorship and tyranny, everything is within that area.

A: The point is, sir, is action possible which does not nourish a centre?

K: Or, can there be no centre?

A: Sir, that cannot be said from our position because we start with a centre. We can honestly, factually say that we know there is a centre, and we know that every activity, including breathing, nourishes that centre.

K: The point is this: the energy that is expanded within the circumference and the centre is a limited energy, a mechanical energy. Do you know, not verbally but actually inside you, that where there is a centre, there must be a circumference and that any action that takes place within that area is limited, fragmented and therefore a wastage of energy?

VA: We have been discussing the circumference and the centre. To realize the self in ourselves would be the first problem.

K: That is the problem, sir. We are selfish entities. We are self-centred human beings, we think about ourselves, our worries, our family—we are the centre. We can move the centre to social work, to political work, but it is still the centre operating.

P: That is a little more subtle to see, because you can concern yourself with something in which you feel the centre is not involved.

K: You may think so. It is 'I' who work for the poor, but I am still working within this limitation.

P: Sir, I want some clarification. It is not the work for the poor which you are questioning?

K: No. It is the identification of myself with the poor, my identification of myself with the nation, identification of myself with God, identification of myself with some ideal and so on, that is the problem.

Apa: I think the question that Pupulji asked was whether this movement of the mind with its habits can be stilled? Can this movement of the mind which is exhausted by identification, by a constant movement, from the centre to the periphery, from the periphery to the centre, can it be silenced? Is there an energy which can gush out, which will silence it or make it irrelevant, make it seem a shadow?

K: I don't quite follow this.

P: It is really like this: we have done everything to understand the nature of this self-centred activity. We have observed, we have meditated, but the centre does not cease, sir.

K: No, because I think we are making a mistake. We don't actually see, perceive in our heart, in our mind, that any action within this periphery, from the centre to the periphery and the circumference, and then from the circumference to the centre, this movement back and forth is a wastage of energy and must be limited and must bring sorrow. Everything within that area is sorrow. We don't see that.

P: Sir, if it is part of our brain cells and if it is the action of our brain cells to constantly throw out these ripples which get caught, which is in a sense self-centred existence, then . . .

K: No, Pupul, the brain needs two things: security and a sense of permanency.

P: Both are provided by the self.

K: That is why it has become very important.

Apa: Sir, the brain is a mechanical, a physical entity in its habit of seeking security or continuance. Now, how do you break out of its habits, its mechanical operations? That is what Pupulji has been hinting at.

K: I don't want to go into that, sir. Any movement to break out, is still within the periphery. Is there an action, a move which is not self-centred?

P: We know states, for instance, when it appears as if the self is not, but then if the seed of self-centred activity is held within the brain cells, it will repeat itself again. Then I say to myself there must be another energy, there must be another quality which will wipe it out.

Apa: Our brains are computers and our behaviour patterns and actions are conditioned and programmed to that. The feed-backs are becoming more and more complicated. Now, sir, what is the energy; is it attention, is it silence, is it exterior, is it interior?

K: Our brain is programmed to function from the centre to the periphery, from the circumference to the centre, this back-and-forth movement. It is programmed for that, it is trained for that, it is conditioned for that. Is it possible to break that momentum of the brain cells?

P: Is there an energy which will, without my volition, wipe out that momentum?

K: Can this momentum, can this programme of the brain, which has been conditioned for millennia, can that stop?

Apa: And de-condition itself.

K: The moment it stops, you have broken it. Now, is there an energy which is not self-centred movement, an energy without a motive, without a cause, an energy which without these would be endless?

P: Yes. And is it possible, I am putting it very tentatively, is it possible to investigate that energy?

K: We are going to.

A: The only instrument we have is attention. So, any energy that you posit must manifest itself as attention. I say attention is the only instrument we have.

P: If I may say so, I don't want to postulate anything. I am asking Krishnaji something which we have not asked before. How do I put it into words?

K: You are asking, is there an energy which is not from the centre, an energy which is without a cause, an energy which is inexhaustible and therefore non-mechanical. We have discovered something. That is, the brain has been conditioned through millennia to move from the centre to the circumference and from the circumference

81

to move to the centre, back and forth, extending it, limiting it and so on. And is there a way of ending that movement? We just now said it ends when there is a stopping, when the plug is pulled out. That is, the brain stops moving in that direction, but if there is any causation for the stopping, you are back again in the circle. Does that answer you? That is, can the brain which has been so conditioned for millennia to act from the centre to the periphery and from the periphery to the centre, can that movement stop? Now, the next question will be: Is it possible? You follow? I think that is a wrong question. When you see the necessity of stopping, when the brain itself sees the necessity of the movement ceasing, it stops. I wonder if I am making myself clear.

Q: Yes. But it starts again. It stops the movement for a while, but then it starts.

K: No, sir, the moment you say you want it again, you are back in the centre.

Q: Probably I want to bring about a permanent stopping.

K: That is greed. If I see the truth of the fact, the moment there is the cessation of this movement, the ending of that movement, the thing is over. It is not a continuous stoppage. When you want it to be continuous, it is a time movement.

Apa: The seeing then is without movement. The seeing has come to an end. That seeing, is it a movement of the centre?

K: Seeing, observing the whole movement of the centre to the circumference, from the circumference to the centre, that movement is 'what is'.

Apa: But that seeing is without any centre.

K: Of course.

Q: So, sir, that seeing is on a different plane, a different dimension altogether.

K: I 'see'. There is perception when you are aware without any choice. Just be aware of this movement. The programme stops. Let us leave that. We will come back to that. Pupul's question is: Is there an energy which is non-mechanical, which has no causation, and therefore an energy that is constantly renewing itself?

VA: That is the energy of death.

K: What do you mean, sir? Death in the sense of ending?

VA: A total ending.

K: You mean a total ending of the periphery.

VA: What I know as myself.

K: Just listen. You said something. The total ending of this movement from the centre to the circumference, that is death, in one sense. Then, is that the energy which is causeless?

VA: It is causeless, sir. It comes, like the blood in the body.

K: I understand. But, is that a supposition, a theory or an actuality?

VA: An actuality.

K: Which means what? That there is no centre from which you are acting?

VA: During that period when that energy is there.

K: No, no. Not periods.

VA: There is a sense of timelessness at that time.

K: Yes, sir. Then, what takes place?

VA: Then again thought comes back.

K: And so, you are back again from the centre to the periphery.

VA: One is afraid of that particular thing happening, not only the wanting it again. One gets afraid of that particular thing happening again because it is like total death.

K: It has happened without your invitation.

VA: Yes.

K: Now, you are inviting it.

VA: I don't know whether I am inviting it or whether I am afraid of it.

K: Afraid or inviting, whatever it is, it is still within the field of this. That is all.

The other question is what Pupulji raised about an endless journey. You want to discuss kundalini?

P: Yes, sir.

K: Sir, first of all, if you really want to discuss, have a dialogue about kundalini, would you forget everything you have heard about it? Would you? We are entering into a subject which is very serious. Are you willing to forget everything you have heard about it, what your gurus have told you about it, or your attempts to awaken it? Can you start with a completely empty state?

Then you have to enquire, really not knowing anything about kundalini. You know what is happening now in America, in Europe. Kundalini centres have been opened by people who say they have had the experience of the awakening of kundalini. Scientists are interested in it today. They feel that by doing certain forms of exercise, breathing, they will awaken the kundalini. It has all become a money-making concern, and it is being given to people who are terribly mischievous.

Q: We just want to know whether there is an energy that can wipe out conditioning.

K: So long as self-centred activity exists, you cannot touch it. That is why I object to any discussion on kundalini or whatever that energy is, because we have not done the spade work. We don't lead a life of correctness and we want to add something new to it and so carry on our mischief.

VA: Even after awakening kundalini, self-centred activity continues.

K: I question whether the kundalini is awakened. I don't know what you mean by it.

84

VA: Sir, we really want to understand this, because it is an actuality sometimes.

P: Do you know of an energy when self-centred activity ends? We assume that this is the source of this endless energy. It may not be.

K: Are you saying the ending of this movement from the centre to the circumference and from the circumference to the centre, the end of that . . .

P: Momentary ending of it . . .

K: No, the ending of it, the complete ending of it—is the release of that energy which is limitless?

P: I don't say that.

K: I am saying that.

P: Which is a very different thing to my saying it.

K: Can we put kundalini energy in its right place? A number of people have the experience of what they call kundalini, which I question. I question whether it is an actual reality or some kind of physiological activity which is then attributed to kundalini. You live an immoral life in the sense of a life of vanity, sex, etc. and then you say that your kundalini is awakened. But your daily life, which is a self-centred life, continues.

P: Sir, if we are going to examine it, let us see how it operates in one. The awakening of kundalini is linked to certain psychic centres located at certain physical parts of the body. That is what is said. The first question I would like to ask is whether that is so? Has the release of this energy, which has no end, anything to do with the psychic centres in the physical parts of the body?

A: Before we go into that, sir, is it not essential to enquire whether the person who acquires that energy is incapable of doing harm.

K: No, sir. Do be careful. How can we say somebody is incapable of doing harm? They say many Indian gurus have done tremendous harm misleading people.

A: That is what I say, sir. I feel that unless the person's heart is cleansed of hate, and his thirst to do harm is completely transmuted, unless that has happened, then this energy can do nothing but more mischief.

K: Achyutji, what Pupulji is asking about is the standard acceptance of the power of this energy going through various centres and the releasing of energy and so on.

A: I say, sir, that before we ask that question, there is in the Indian tradition a word which I think is very valuable. That word is 'adhikar'. Adhikar means that the person must cleanse himself sufficiently before he can pose this question to himself. It is a question of cleansing.

K: Are you saying that unless there is a stoppage of this movement from the centre to the circumference and from the circumference to the centre, that Pupulji's question is not valid?

A: I think so. I will use another word, the Buddhist word is 'sheela'. It is really the same. The word 'adhikar' used by the Hindus and the word 'sheela' used by the Buddhist really mean the same thing.

P: I take it that when one asks the question, there is a depth of self-knowing with which one asks. It is not possible to investigate the self which also releases energy, if one's life has not gone through a degree of inner balance, otherwise what K says has no meaning. When one listens to Krishnaji, one receives at the depth to which one has exposed oneself, and therefore I think it is right to ask the question. Why is this question more dangerous than any other question? Why is it more dangerous than inquiring into what is thought, what is meditation, what is this, what is that? To the mind which will comprehend, it will comprehend this and that. To the mind which will not comprehend, it will comprehend neither. To the mind which wants to misuse, it will misuse anything.

K: Unless your life, your daily life is a completely nonself-centred way of living, the other cannot possibly come in.

VA: There is arising of energy—there is delight at first, then fear.

S: We would like to know why that energy creates fear.

VA: Fear comes later. One experiences death and everything vanishes. You are alive again and you are surprised that you are alive again. You find the world again, and your thoughts, and your possessions and desires and the whole world slowly come back.

K: Would you call that, sir, the awakening of kundalini?

VA: I don't know, sir.

K: But why do you label it as the awakening of kundalini?

VA: For a few days after that, for a period of a month, the whole life changes. Sex vanishes, desires vanish.

K: Yes, sir, I understand. But you do come back to it again.

VA: One comes back to it because one doesn't understand.

K: That is what I am saying, sir. When there is a coming back to something, I question whether you have had that energy.

P: Why has this question awakened so many ripples? Most people go through a great deal of psychic experiences in the process of self-knowing. One also understands, at least one has understood because one has listened to Krishnaji, that all psychic experiences when they arise, have to be put aside.

K: Is that understood? Psychic experience must be totally put aside.

A: We put them aside, not only give no importance to them.

VA: Some new passages do get opened in the body, and the energy keeps rising in those passages whenever it is required.

K: Sir, why do you call it something extraordinary? Why do we attribute something extraordinary to this? I am just suggesting, it may be that you have become very sensitive. That is all. Very acutely sensitive.

VA: I have more energy.

K: Sensitivity has more energy. But why do you call it extraordinary, kundalini, this, that or the other?

P: The real problem is to what extent is your life totally changed. I mean the only meaning of awakening is if there is a totally new way of looking, a new way of living, a new way of relationship.

Q: Sir, I want to ask a question. Taking for granted that one is leading a holistic life, is there something like kundalini?

K: Sir, are you living a holistic life?

Q: No.

K: Therefore, don't ask that question.

P: I am asking from a totally different point. As it is understood, kundalini is the awakening of certain psychic energies which exist at certain physical points in the human body, and that it is possible to awaken the psychic energies through various practices which then, as they go through these various psycho-physical states and centres, transmute consciousness, and when they finally break through, they pierce through self-centred activity. This must be the basic meaning of the whole thing.

Apa: Mescalin can do it; you can do it.

P: I am just asking Krishnaji whether there is an energy which, on awakening, not being awakened, but on awakening completely wipes out the centre.

K: I would put it the other way. Unless the self-centred movement stops, the other can't be.

A: I say that the whole Hatha yoga tradition has engendered a belief that by manipulating these centres, you can do things to yourself. The whole idea is based on a wrong belief.

P: Wipe out everything.

A: We should wipe it out.

P: As it does not seem possible to proceed with this discussion, may I put another question? What is the nature of the field which needs to be prepared, to be able to receive that which is limitless?

K: Are you cultivating the soil of the brain, of the mind, in order to receive it?

P: I understand your question. But I can neither say yes nor no to it.

K: Then, why call it energy and bring the word 'soil'? Prepare, work at it. We live a life of contradiction, conflict, misery. I want to find out if it can end sorrow, the whole of human sorrow and enquire into the nature of compassion.

S: Is there any other way of living in which compassion is also part of cultivating the self? Why are you asking this question, why do you want to cultivate the soil?

K: I say as long as you have motive to cultivate that soil in order to receive that energy, you will never receive it.

S: What is the motive, sir? It is the whole prison. To see the whole prison and ask whether there is any other way out of this, is it a motive? Then, one gets caught in a circle, in a trap.

K: No, you haven't listened. I live a life of torture, misery, confusion. That is my basic feeling and can that end? There is no motive.

S: Here there is no motive. But you are also asking a further question.

K: No. I don't have further questions, only that first question. Can that whole process end? Only then can I answer the other questions, which have tremendous significance.

P: What is the nature of the soil of the human mind which has to be cultivated to receive the other? You tell me that is also a wrong question. You say I am in conflict, I am suffering and I see that a life of conflict and suffering has no end.

K: That is all. If it cannot end, then the other enquiry and investigation, and the wanting to awaken the other in order to wipe this out is a wrong process.

P: Obviously.

K: It is asking an outside agency to come and clear up your house. I say in the process of clearing the house, this house, there are a great many things that are going to happen. You will have clairvoyance, the so-called 'siddhis' and all the rest of it. They will all happen. But if you are caught in them, you cannot proceed further. If you are not caught in them, the heavens are open to you. You are asking, Pupul, is there a soil that has to be prepared, not in order to receive that, but the soil has to be prepared? Prepare, work at that, clean the house so completely that there isn't the shadow of escape. Then, we can ask, what is the state we are all talking about. If you are doing that, preparing, working at the ending of sorrow, not letting go, if you are working at that and you come along and say is there something known as kundalini power, then I am willing to listen.

A: Sir, the reason why I objected is that in the Hatha yoga Pradipika text we make a statement that this investigation into kundalini is in order to strengthen you in your search.

K: For God's sake, Achyutji, are you working at clearing up the house?

A: Definitely.

K: Now, what is the question? Is there an energy which is non-mechanistic, which is endless, renewing itself? I say there is. Most definitely. But it is not what you call kundalini. The body must be sensitive. If you are working, clearing up the house, the body becomes very sensitive. The body then has its own intelligence, not the intelligence which the mind dictates to the body. Therefore, the body becomes extraordinarily sensitive, not sensitive to its desires, or sensitive to wanting something, but it becomes sensitive *per se*. Right? Then, what happens? If you really want me to go into it, I'll do so. The people who speak of the awakening of kundalini, I question. They have not worked at the other, but say they have awakened kundalini. Therefore, I question their ability, their truth. I am not antagonistic, but I am questioning it. A man who eats meat, wants publicity, wants this and that and says his kundalini is awakened, I say it is nonsense. There must be a cleansing of this house all the time. Then Pupul says, 'Can we talk about an energy which I feel must exist?', not theoretically but of which she has had a glimpse, the feeling of it, an energy that is endless; and K comes along and says 'yes', there is such a thing. There is an energy which is renewing itself all the time, which is not mechanistic, which has no cause, which has no beginning and therefore no ending. It is an eternal movement. I say there is. What value has it to the listener? I say 'yes' and you listen to me. I say to myself what value has that to you? Will you go off into that and not clear up the house?

P: That means, sir, that to the person who enquires, it is the cultivation of the soil which is the ending of suffering, which is essential.

K: The only job. Nothing else. It is the most sacred thing, therefore you can't invite it. And you are all inviting it.

Clearing the house demands tremendous discipline, not the discipline of control, suppression and obedience, you follow? In itself it demands tremendous attention. When you give your complete attention, then you will see a totally different kind of thing taking place, an energy in which there is no repetition, and energy that isn't coming and going. It is not as though I have it one day and a month later I don't have it. It implies, keeping the mind completely empty. Can you do that?

VA: For a while.

K: No, no. I have asked: Can the mind keep itself empty? Then, there is that energy. You don't even have to ask for it. When there is space, it is empty and therefore full of energy. So, in cleansing, in ending the things of the house, of sorrow, can the mind be completely empty, without any motive, without any desire? When you are working at this, keeping the house clean, other things come

91

naturally. It isn't you who are preparing the soil for that. That is meditation.

P: And the nature of that is the transformation of the human mind.

K: You see as Apa Saheb was saying, we are programmed to centuries of conditioning. When there is the stopping of it, there is an ending of it. If you pull the plug out of the computer, it can't function any more. Now, the question is: Can that centre, which is selfishness, end? And not keep on and on? Can that centre end? When that ends, there is no movement of time. That is all. When the movement of the mind from the centre to the periphery stops, time stops. When there is no movement of selfishness, there is a totally different kind of movement.

The Central Root of Fear

P: You have said, Krishnaji, that intelligence is the greatest security in the facing of fear. The problem is: In a crisis, when fear from the unconscious floods you, where is the place for intelligence? Intelligence demands negation of that which comes in the way. It demands listening, seeing and observation. But when the whole being is flooded by uncontrollable fear, fear which has a cause, but the cause of which is not immediately discernable, in that state where is the place for intelligence? How does one deal with the primeval, archetypal fears which lie at the very base of the human psyche? One of these fears is the destruction of the self, the fear of not being.

K: What is it we are exploring together?

P: How does one deal with fear? You have still not answered that. You have talked of intelligence being the greatest security. It is so; but when fear floods you, where is intelligence?

K: You are saying that at the moment of a great wave of fear, intelligence is not. And how can one deal with that wave of fear at that moment? Is that the question?

S: One sees fear like the branches of a tree. But we deal with these fears one by one and there is no freedom from fear. Is there a quality that sees fear without the branches?

K: K said, 'Do we see the leaves, the branches, or do we go to the very root of fear?'

S: Can we go to the root of each single branch of fear?

K: Let us find out.

P: You may come to see the whole, through one fear.

93

K: I understand. You are saying there are conscious and unconscious fears and the unconscious fears become extraordinarily strong at moments and at those moments intelligence is not in operation. How can one deal with those waves of uncontrollable fear. Is that it?

P: These fears seem to take on a material form. It is a physical thing which overpowers you.

K: It upsets you neurologically, biologically. Let us explore. Fear exists, consciously or at depths, when there is a sense of loneliness, when there is a feeling of complete abandonment by others, a sense of complete isolation, the sense of not being, a feeling of utter helplessness. And at those moments, when deep fear arises, obviously intelligence is not and there is ungovernable, uninvited fear.

P: One may feel that one has faced the fears which are known but unconsciously one is swamped.

K: That is what we are saying. Discuss it. One can deal with physical, conscious fears. The outskirts of intelligence can deal with them.

P: You can even allow those fears to flower.

K: And then in that very flowering there is intelligence. Now how do you deal with the other? Why does the unconscious—we will use that word 'unconscious' for the time being—hold these fears? Or does the unconscious invite these fears? Does it hold them, do they exist in the traditional depths of the unconscious; or is it a thing that the unconscious gathers from the environment? Now, why does the unconscious hold fears at all? Are they all an inherent part of the unconscious, of the racial, traditional history of man? Are they in the inherited genes? How do you deal with the problem?

P: Can we discuss the second one, which is the gathering of fear from the environment?

K: First of all, let us deal with the first one. Why does the unconscious hold them at all? Why do we consider the deeper layers of consciousness as the storehouse, as the residue of fear? Are they imposed by the culture in which we live, by the conscious mind which, not being able to deal with fear, has pushed it down and therefore it remains at the level of the unconscious? Or is it that the mind with all its content has not resolved its problems and is frightened of not being able to resolve them? I want to find out what is the significance of the unconscious. When you said these waves of fear come, I say they are always there, but, in a crisis, you become aware of them.

S: They exist in consciousness. Why do you say they are in the unconscious?

K: First of all consciousness is made up of its content. Without its content there is no consciousness. One of its contents is this basic fear and the conscious mind never tackles it; it is there, but it never says, 'I must deal with it'. In moments of crisis that part of consciousness is awakened and is frightened. But fear is always there.

P: I don't think it is so simple. Is fear not a part of man's cultural inheritance?

K: Fear is always there. Is it part of the cultural inheritance? Or is it possible that one is born in a country, in a culture that does not admit fear?

P: There is no such culture.

K: Of course there is no such culture. And so I am asking myself, is fear part of culture or is it inherent in man? Fear is a sense of not being, as it exists in the animal, as it exists in every living thing; the fear of being destroyed.

P: The self-preservative instinct which takes the form of fear.

K: Is it that the whole structure of the cells is frightened of not being? That exists in every living thing. Even the little ant is afraid of not being. We see fear is there, part of human existence, and one becomes tremendously aware of it in a crisis. How does one deal with it at that moment when the surge of fear comes about? Why do we wait for the crisis? I am just asking.

P: You can't avoid it.

K: Just a minute. We say it is always there, it is part of our human structure. The biological, psychological, the whole structure of the being is frightened. Fear is there, it is part of the tiniest living thing, the minutest cell. Why do we wait for a crisis to come and bring it out? That is a most irrational acceptance of it. I say, why should I have a crisis to deal with fear?

P: Otherwise it is non-existent; I can face some fears intelligently. One faces fear of death. It is possible to face it with intelligence. Is it possible to face other fears intelligently?

K: You say you can face these fears intelligently. I question whether you face them intelligently. I question whether you can have intelligence before you have resolved fear. Intelligence comes only when fear is not. Intelligence is light and you cannot deal with darkness when light is not. Light exists only when darkness is not. I am questioning whether you can deal with fear intelligently when fear exists. I say you cannot. You may rationalize it, you may see the nature of it, avoid it or go beyond it, but that is not intelligence.

P: I would say intelligence lies in an awareness of fear arising, in leaving it alone, in not shaping it, in not turning away from it, and so to the dissolution of fear. But you say that where intelligence is, fear does not arise.

N: Will fear not arise?

K: But we don't allow fear to arise.

N: I think fear arises. We don't allow it to flower.

K: You see, I am questioning altogether the whole response to a crisis. Fear is there; why do you need a crisis to awaken it? You say a crisis takes place and you wake up. A word, a gesture, a look, a movement, a thought, those are challenges that you say bring it out. I am asking: Why do we wait for the crisis? We are investigating. Do you know what that word 'investigate' means?—'to trace out'. Therefore, we are tracing out, we are not saying this, that or the other. We are following it, and I am asking: Why do I wait for a crisis? A gesture, a thought, a word, a look, a whisper; any of these are challenges.

N: I don't look for the crisis. The only thing I am aware of is, it arises and I am paralysed.

K: You get paralysed, why? Therefore for you, challenge is necessary. Why don't you contact fear before the challenge? You say crisis awakens fear. Crisis includes thought, gesture, word, whisper, a look, a letter. Is it a challenge which awakens fear? I say to myself, why should one not awaken to it without a challenge? If fear is there, it must be awake; or is it dormant? And if it is dormant, why is it dormant? Is the conscious mind frightened that fear may awaken? Has it put it to sleep and refused to look at it?

Let us go slowly, we are tracing a rocket. Has the conscious mind been frightened of looking at fear and therefore it keeps fear quiet? Or fear is there, awake, and the conscious mind won't let it flower? Do you admit that fear is part of human life, of existence?

P: Sir, fear has no independent existence apart from the outer experience, without the stimuli of outer experience.

K: Wait, I question it, I don't accept it. You are saying without the outer stimuli, it is not. If it is true to you, it must be so for me, because I am a human being.

P: I include in that both the outer and the inner stimuli.

K: I don't divide the outer and the inner. It is all one movement.

P: Fear has no existence apart from the stimuli.

K: You are moving away, Pupul.

P: You are asking: Why don't you look at it, why don't you face it?

K: I say to myself: 'Must I wait for a crisis for this fear to awaken?' That's all my question. If it is there, who has put it to sleep? Is it because the conscious mind cannot resolve it? The conscious mind is concerned with resolving it, and not being able to do so, it puts it to sleep, squashes it. And the conscious mind is shaken when a crisis takes place and fear arises. So I am saying to myself, why should the conscious mind supress fear?

S: Sir, the instrument of the conscious mind is analysis, the capacity of recognition. With these instruments it is inadequate to deal with fear.

K: It can't deal with it. But what is required is real simplicity, not analysis. The conscious mind cannot deal with fear, therefore it says I want to avoid it, I can't look at it. Look what you are doing. You are waiting for a crisis to awaken it, and the conscious mind is all the time avoiding crisis. It is avoiding, reasoning, rationalizing. We are masters at this game. Therefore I say to myself, if fear is there, it is awake. You cannot put to sleep a thing that is part of our inheritance. The conscious mind only thinks that it has put fear to sleep. The conscious mind is shaken when a crisis takes place. Therefore deal with it differently. That's all my point. Is this true? The basic fear is of non-existence, a sense of complete fear of uncertainty, of not being, of dying. Why does the mind not bring that fear out and move with it? Why should it wait for a crisis? Are you lazy and therefore you haven't got the energy to go to the root of it? Is what I am saying irrational?

P: It is not irrational. I am trying to see if it is valid.

K: We say that every living thing is frightened of not being, not surviving. Fear is part of our blood cells. Our whole being is frightened of not being, frightened of dying, frightened of being killed. So fear of not being is part of our whole psychological, as well as biological structure, and I am asking myself why is a crisis necessary, why should challenge become important? I object to challenge. I want to be ahead of challenge, not behind challenge.

P: One cannot participate in what you are saying.

K: Why can't you? I am going to show it to you. I know I am going to die, but I have intellectualized, rationalized death. Therefore when I say my mind is far ahead of death, it is not. It is only far ahead of thought—which is not being far ahead.

P: Let us take the actuality of it. One faces death and one feels one is a step ahead and one moves on and suddenly realizes that one is not ahead of it.

K: I understand that. It is all the result of a challenge, whether it took place yesterday or a year ago.

P: So the question is: With what instrument, with what energy, from what dimension does one see; and what does one see?

K: I want to be clear. Fear is part of our structure, our inheritance. Biologically, psychologically, the brain cells are frightened of not being. And thought says I am not going to look at this thing. And so when the challenge takes place, thought cannot end it.

P: What do you mean when you say, 'Thought says I don't want to look at it'?

N: It wants to look at it also.

K: Thought cannot look at the ending of itself. It can only rationalize about it. I am asking you why does the mind wait for a challenge? Is it necessary? If you say it is necessary, then you are waiting for it.

P: I say I don't know. I only know that challenge arises and fear arises.

K: No, challenge awakens fear. Let us stick to that, and I say to you, why do you wait for a challenge for this to awaken?

P: Your question is a paradox. Would you say that you don't wait for the challenge but evoke the challenge?

K: No, I am opposed to challenge altogether. You are missing my point. My mind will not accept challenge at any time. Challenge is not necessary to awaken. To say I am asleep and that challenge is necessary to awaken me, is a wrong statement.

P: No, sir, that's not what I am saying.

K: So it is awake. Now what sleeps? Is it the conscious mind? Or is the unconscious mind asleep and are there some parts of the mind that are awake?

P: When I am awake, I am awake.

N: Do you invite fear?

K: If you are awake, no challenge is necessary. So you reject challenge. If as we said it is part of our life that we should die, then one is awake all the time.

P: Not all the time. You are not conscious of fear. But it is there all the time under the carpet. But you don't look at it.

K: I say it is under the carpet, lift it and look. It is there. That's all my point. It is there and awake. So it does not need a challenge to make it awake. I am frightened all the time of not being, of dying, of not achieving. That is the basic fear of our life, of our blood and it is there, always watching, guarding, protecting itself. But it is very much awake. It is never a moment asleep. Therefore, challenge is not necessary. What you do about it and how you deal with it comes later.

P: That is the fact.

A: Seeing all this, don't you accept the factor of non-attention?

K: I said it is awake, I am not talking of attention.

A: Fear is active, operating.

K: It is like a snake in the room, it is always there. I may look elsewhere, but it is there. The conscious mind is concerned how to deal with it, and as it can't deal with it, it moves away. The conscious mind then receives a challenge and tries to face it. Can you face a living thing? That does not need a challenge. But because the conscious mind has blinded itself against fear, the challenge is needed. Right, Pupul?

N: When you think of it, it is just a thought; still that shadow is in the mind.

K: Trace it, don't jump to conclusions. You have jumped to conclusions. My mind refuses challenge. The conscious mind will not allow challenge to awaken it. It is awake. But you admit challenge. I don't admit challenge. It is not within my experience.

The next question is, when the conscious mind is awake to fear, it cannot invite something that is there. Go step by step. Don't conclude at any second. So, the conscious mind knows it is there, fully awake. Then what are we going to do next?

P: There lies inadequacy.

N: I am awake.

K: You are missing the whole point. It is the conscious mind that is frightened of this. When it is awake, it is not frightened. In itself, it is not frightened. The ant is not frightened. If it is squashed, it is squashed. It is the conscious mind that says I am frightened of this, of not being. But when I meet with an accident, an aeroplane crashes, there is no fear. At the moment of death I say, 'Yes, I know now what it means to die'. But the conscious mind with all its thoughts says, 'My god, I am going to die, I will not die, I must not die, I will protect myself'; that is the thing that is frightened. Have you never watched an ant? It is never frightened: if somebody kills it, it dies. Now you see something.

N: Sir, have you ever seen an ant? If you put a piece of paper in front of the ant, it dodges it.

K: It wants to survive, but it is not thinking about surviving. So we will come back to it. Thought creates fear: it is only thought that says, 'I will die, I am lonely. I have not fulfilled.' See this: that is timeless eternity, that is real eternity. See how extraordinary it is. Why should I be frightened if fear is part of my being? It is only when thought says that life must be different, that there is fear. Can the mind be completely motionless? Can the mind be completely stable? Then that thing comes. When that thing is awake, what then is the central root of fear?

P: Has it ever happened to you, sir?

K: Several times, many times, when the mind is completely stable, without any recoil, neither accepting not denying, nor rationalizing nor escaping, there is no movement of any kind. We have got at the root of it, have we not?

101

The Chattering Mind

M: I want to discuss the problem of the chattering mind. What makes our minds chatter? Where does the mind get the energy and what is the purpose of that chattering? It is a constant operation. Every moment it is murmuring.

P: Isn't it the very nature of the mind?

M: That does not explain it, does not offer any remedy.

P: It must operate in order to exist.

M: It is not a 'must'. There is no 'must'. The mind chatters all the time and the energy devoted to that purpose fills a major part of our life.

K: Why does the mind chatter, what is its purpose?

M: There is no purpose. As I watch the brain, I see that the chattering happens only in the brain, it is a brain activity; a current flows up and down, but it is chaotic, meaningless and purposeless. The brain wears itself out by its own activity. One can see that it is tiring to the brain, but it does not stop.

K: Is this worth pursuing?

P: If you take the process of thought continuous, without beginning and without end, then why should one differentiate between the chattering and the thought process itself?

M: Our awareness or attention is absolutely wasted on it. We are aware of something that has absolutely no meaning. It is the neurotic function of the brain and our time, our awareness, attention, our best efforts are wasted.

P: Would you say there is meaningful thought activity and chattering?

K: Your mind chatters, why?

M: Because I cannot stop it.

K: Is it habit? Is it a fear of not being occupied with something?

A: It is an extra-volitional act.

M: It looks like a simple automatic activity. It just is there, there is no feeling, there is nothing.

K: Your have not understood what I mean. The mind apparently needs to be occupied with something.

M: The mind is occupied all the time.

K: The mind is occupied with something and if it is not occupied, it feels vacant, it feels empty and therefore it resorts to chattering. I am just asking, is it habit or is it the fear of not being occupied?

M: It is a habit, an ingrained habit.

K: I wonder if it is a habit?

P: There is what we call meaningful thinking, directed thinking, thinking which is logical, which is analytical, which is concerned with the solution of problems. Chattering is not a conscious thing. In a non-aware state there is a continual movement of the mind throwing up reflexes, coming out with the accumulation of the rubbish the mind has acquired over the years and it keeps on throwing out and suddenly you awaken and say your mind is chattering. We give weight to what we call meaningful activity as against what we call chattering. Is this weight valid?

K: Why is it chattering?

P: It chatters; there is no 'why' to it.

K: He wants to find out why it chatters. Is it just like water flowing, like water running out of the tap?

M: It is a mental leakage.

P: It indicates to me, that my mind is not alive.

K: Why do you object to a chattering mind?

M: Loss of energy, loss of time; common sense says that what is going on is useless.

P: We are back in the intermediate stage—we are neither here nor there. And it is not only the mind chattering, but also the awareness of the chattering, which is an indication of inadequacy.

K: Drop attention, awareness, for the moment. I am just asking you why does the mind chatter? Is it a habit or does the mind need to be occupied with something? And when it is not occupied with what it thinks it should be occupied, we call it chattering. Why should not the occupation be chattering also? I am occupied with my house. You are occupied with your God, with your work, with your business, with your wife, with your sex, with your children, with your property. The mind needs to be occupied with something and therefore when it is not occupied, it may feel a sense of emptiness and therefore chatters. I don't see any problem in this. I don't see the great issue in this, unless you want to stop it chattering.

M: If chattering were not oppressive, there would be no problem.

K: You want to stop it, you want to put an end to it. So the question is not 'why' but what for?

M: Can a chattering mind be put an end to?

K: Can a chattering mind come to an end? I don't know what you call chattering. I am questioning. When you are occupied with your business, that is also chattering. I want to find out what you call chattering. I say that any occupation, with myself, with my God, with my wife, with my husband, with my children, money, property or position, the whole of that is chattering. Why exclude all that and say the other is chattering?

M: I am only talking about what I observe.

P: Because the chattering we speak of has no rationality.

K: It has no relationship to your daily activity. There is no rationality. It is not related to daily life. It has nothing to do with your everyday demands and so it chatters and that is what you call chattering. We all know that.

P: Do you do that?

K: That does not matter. Don't bother about me.

A: Sir, our normal thinking has coherence to a context. Chattering is that activity of the mind which has no coherence to any context. Therefore we call it unmeaningful because we can break through the context, but when the activity of the mind is unconnected then it has no coherence.

K: Is chattering a rest to the mind?

A: No, sir.

K: Wait, sir, not so quick. Listen Achyutji, I want to ask you; you are occupied with your daily work, conscious, rational, irrational, and chattering may be a release from all that.

B: Would chattering bear the same relationship as the dream to the waking state?

K: No. I wouldn't put it that way. My muscles have been exercised all day and I relax, and chattering may be a form of relaxation.

A: It may be totally irrelevant. But it dissipates energy.

K: Does it?

A: Relaxation should not dissipate energy. Relaxation is an activity which comes into being after you have exhausted your energy and then are resting.

K: Chattering, you say, is a wastage of energy and you want to stop it.

A: It is not a question of wanting to stop it. The problem is that the mind that is wasting its energy in chattering should be put to something worthwhile. One can do some kind of *japa*, but that will again be a mechanical thing, it will solve no problem. We come back to understanding how this chattering process is going on. We don't understand it at all. It is extra-volitional.

K: Would your mind stop chattering if it was fully occupied? Just listen, sir; if there is no empty space, if there is no space or if the whole mind is full of space, will it chatter? It is not a matter of what word you use—space, full, totally empty, or completely without any occupation. Does the mind then chatter? Or does chattering take place only when there is some little space which is not covered? Do you know what I mean? When the room is completely full, would there be any movement at all? When the mind is completely full and there is no space, would there be any movement at all which you call chattering? I don't know if I am conveying something.

M: It is hypothetical.

K: In the sense that our minds are partly full, partly occupied and the unoccupied part is chattering.

M: You are identifying with the unoccupied mind.

K: I am not saying that. I am asking, I want to find out why the mind chatters. Is it a habit?

M: It looks like habit.

K: Why has the habit arisen?

M: There is no reason as far as we know.

K: I don't mind it chattering, but you object to its chattering. I am not sure it is a wastage of energy. Is it a habit? If it is a habit, then how does that habit come to an end? That is the only thing that you are concerned with. How does a habit come to an end—any habit, smoking, drinking, over-eating?

M: Unless you know something from your own experience, it is like talking to a child. It usually comes to an end by intensely looking at it.

K: Will chattering stop when you intensely look at it?

M: That is the wonder, it does not.

K: I am not sure it does not. If I intensely observe smoking, paying attention to all the movement of smoking, it withers away. So, why can't chattering wither away?

M: Because it is automatic, smoking is not automatic.

K: It is not automatic? It has become automatic.

M: Let us not refer to the beginnings. There are no beginnings. I cannot trace any beginning to chattering. It is peculiarly automatic. It is an automatic shivering of the brain. I see only the brain shivering, murmuring and I cannot do anything.

P: All other systems that deal with this peripheral movement of chattering say that it must end before one can get down to doing anything else.

M: To end it, you repeat mantras, bring some uniformity, some monotony to the mind. But chattering is not monotonous, the content changes.

K: That is interesting: the content changes.

P: It is completely disjointed. The basic problem is that so long as the thinking process fills the major portion of consciousness, there will be both directed thinking and chattering. I don't think it is possible to get rid of one and keep the other.

A: I would say that there is another approach to this, that our mind functions at different levels and chattering is that movement in which all these levels get jumbled.

P: I don't think it is so, Achyutji. I don't think the levels get jumbled. The conscious movement of thinking is when the thinker draws on thought to build a premise and moves from there logically. In the field of the irrational, the chattering, many, many things take place which the rational mind does not understand. But I was wondering whether the two are not counterparts of each other and whether one can exist without the other.

107

B: We object to chattering apparently, but we don't object to directed occupation.

P: That is what I am saying. I say, as long as this is there, the other will also be.

A: I question that.

P: Let us discuss it. I wonder whether this is not a reflex of the other.

B: The mind knows directed occupation, the mind also knows chattering, a non-directional chattering. Does the mind know space or emptiness?

P: Where does space come in?

B: Because Krishnaji brought in space.

P: Don't put it that way. If one exists, the other will exist. That is what I would like to go into.

A: No. It is possible for a person to be efficient in the doing of any single job to which he is directed. That is directed activity. You say that any person who is capable of directed activity must also have the lunatic fringe of chattering all the time.

P: Directed activity does not mean a purely technological function; there is also the psychological activity which is directed. As long as the psychological, emotional activity is directed, the other remains.

A: You see, sir, the directed activity can be understood as either a projection of the centre or that which strengthens the centre. So directed activity can be traced to a source, that source is a centre or it creates the source.

K: How do you stop chattering? That is what he is interested in.

P: If I may pursue it with Achyutji, he says that it is possible that there can be a state of directed thinking both at the functional level and at the psychological level within the mind; and there is also chattering.

108

A: That is directed activity. I know its source, I know its intent.

P: Directed activity—do I really know the source?

A: That is how the centre sustains itself. This is the centre.

P: When I want to explore and find the root of that, I find neither the root, nor do I find the source.

A: I don't find it either. I say this is a self-sustaining activity out of which the centre gets strengthened, fed. Here is a channel of movement which seems to be even unrelated to that.

M: So you divide the flow of the mind into chattering and non-chattering.

P: How do you know that?

K: He says chattering is a wastage of energy.

D: Why do you say that? How does he know?

K: Oh, yes. It is so irrational, so illogical, sloppy, it is all over the place.

D: Don't we know that all rational effort ends in nothing?

K: Wait, wait.

M: Right or wrong, why choose? There are three movements of the mind—intended, non-intended and the mixed. I am not quarrelling with the intended. My quarrel is with the non-intended. Can I do away with the non-intended movement?

K: That is all that we are concerned with. My mind chatters. I want to turn to any thing to stop it chattering, I want to stop it, because I see it is irrational, tawdry. How is it to come to an end?

M: All I can do is to look at it. As long as I can look at it, it stops.

K: But it will return later. I want to stop it for good. Now, how am I to do it? Instead of being occupied with a directed, intended movement, now I have occupied myself with stopping chattering. I want to get at this.

B: I don't object to being occupied with money, with a hundred different kinds of things. I think that is all right. Why does the wretched mind chatter? I want to stop that.

A: Looking at directed activity helps me to understand the ego process, the centre, how it all gets tied up. The exploration always leads to a little more clarity.

K: Achyutji, I want to stop chattering and I see it is a wastage of energy. What am I to do? How am I to stop it for good?

P: I feel that as long as you are looking at any process of the mind, whether it is directed action or non-directed action, you are trapped.

K: Why do I object to chattering? You say you are wasting energy, but you are wasting energy in ten different directions. Sir, I don't object to my mind chattering. I don't mind wasting a little bit of energy because I am wasting energy in so many directions. Why do I object to chattering?

M: Because I waste energy.

K: So you are against wasting energy on a particular kind of work. I object to wasting energy on any account.

M: It is a questionable point: what is waste of energy and what is not?

A: I would also like to make sure that we are not shirking a very difficult problem.

P: There are two ways of looking at this: the one way is of saying, how can I solve the problem? The other, why does one differentiate between the directed and non-directed?

A: I don't object to that.

K: Frydman objects to that.

M: In any case, whenever my mind is in a state of chattering, there is anguish, there is despair.

K: Sir, let us stick to one thing at a time. You say it is a wastage of energy. We waste energy in so many ways.

M: It is a most unpleasant way.

K: You don't want the unpleasant waste of energy, but you would rather have the pleasant.

M: Of course.

K: So, you are objecting to the waste of energy which is unpleasant. I will approach it differently. I am not concerned with whether my mind chatters or not. What is important is not whether there is movement, not-directed, directed, intended or not-intended, but that the mind is very steady, rock-steady and then the problem does not exist; the mind does not chatter. Let it chatter.

P: I have to ask you a question. Are you first aware and then you speak? Are you aware of the word formations in the mind?

K: What is this? Wait, wait, hold on to that. I would approach the question quite differently. If the mind is completely rock-steady, then a word passing over it, somebody spilling water on it or a bird making a mess on it, it brushes it off. That is the only way I would approach it. Find out if the mind is rock-steady and then a little wave, a little rain, a little movement does not matter. But you are approaching it from the point of trying to stop wastage of energy, irrational wastage, unintended wastage, and I say unintended or intended wastage is taking place all around you, all the time. Sir, to me the problem is very simple. Is the mind totally steady?

I know the mind chatters, I know there is wastage of energy in so many directions, intended or unintended, conscious or unconscious. I say leave it alone, don't be so terribly concerned about it, look at it in a different way.

P: Does your mind operate in thought at all, in thought and word formation moving across the mind?

K: No.

P: Do your brain cells ever spill out words which indicate a chattering mind?

M: He does not know what he is going to say next but he says something and it makes sense. Here is a man who is completely empty.

P: So your consciousness is really empty?

K: This does not lead us very far. Let us drop that.

B: Sir, you approach the issue from two different positions: one, you say look at fragmentation, look what happens; then you suddenly take a jump, and you say leave it and you ask is there a mind that is imperturbable?

K: I don't think the problem of chattering will be stopped the other way.

B: What is the relationship of the two approaches?

K: I don't think there is any. Look, the mind is chattering and we have discussed it for half an hour, talked about it from different points of view. The mind still goes on fragmentarily, wanting to resolve the problem by looking at it and by various means. I listen to it all and I say this does not seem to be the answer. It does not seem to complete the picture and I see it is so because our minds are so unsteady. The mind has not got deep roots of in-depth steadiness and therefore it chatters. So that may be it. From the observation of 'what is', I have not jumped away, I have watched it.

B: You have not jumped away, we have dealt with the parts in ourselves, whereas you have collected the whole thing together.

K: That is how I would operate, if my mind were chattering. I know it is wastage of energy. I look at it and some other factor comes into it—the fact that my mind is not steady at all. So I would pursue that rather than the chattering.

P: When you say that if my mind chatters, I would pursue the fact that it is not stable, how would you tackle it? Pursue what?

112

K: That would be my concern, not my chattering. I see as long as the mind is not steady, there must be chattering. So I am not concerned about chattering. So I am going to find out what is the feeling and the quality of a mind that is completely steady? That is all. I have moved away from chattering.

M: You have moved away from 'what is' to 'what is not'.

K: No. I have not moved away to 'what is not'. I know my mind chatters. That's a fact. I know it is irrational, involuntary, unintended, a wastage of energy; I also know I am wasting energy in ten different ways. To gather all the wastage of energy is impossible. You spill mercury and there are hundreds of little droplets all over the place. To collect them is also wastage of energy. So I see, there must be a different way. The mind, not being steady, chatters. My enquiry now is: What is the nature and structure of steadiness?

M: The steadiness is not there with me.

K: I don't know it. I am going to enquire. I am going to come to it, I am going to find out. You say steadiness is the opposite of restlessness. I say steadiness is not the opposite of restlessness, because the opposite always contains the opposite of itself. Therefore it is not the opposite. I started with chattering and I see the wastage of energy and I also see the mind wastes energy in so many ways and I cannot collect all these wastages and make it whole. So I leave that problem. I understand it, it may be that the chattering will go on, all the wastage will go on in different directions as long as the mind is not rock-steady. That is not a verbal statement. It is an understanding of a state that has come into being by discarding the enquiry how to gather the wastage. I am not concerned about the wastage of energy.

M: I understand that when there is the rock-steady state of mind, then there will be no wastage.

K: No, no.

B: There has always been this problem that with us, the negative

113

is transformed into the positive by the mind. The negative does not naturally transform itself, you will say. But what would you do about it?

K: I don't know. I am not bothered about it.

P: But you also say that it will be your concern.

B: When he says that the negative is the positive, the negative observation is instantly the positive. The negative goes through this process.

K: Attention is applied in a different direction. Instead of how to stop the wastage, it is now directed to the understanding of what it means to be steady.

B: But it is not a mental direction.

K: No, obviously not. It is not a verbal direction. I think that is really quite important. What is the nature of a steady mind? Can we discuss that, not the verbal description of a steady mind?

P: What is the nature of a steady mind?

M: Are you talking about being momentarily steady?

P: I don't understand a state of mind which is momentarily steady.

K: He said: 'Is it temporary or permanent?' I don't like the word 'permanent'.

P: But what is the nature of a steady mind?

K: Don't you know it?

M: By your grace we all know it.

P: I would say that, but that still would not stop either the chattering or the thinking process.

K: He said the sea is very deep, it is very steady, a few waves come and go, and you don't care, but if you care then you remain there.

P: When you find yourself remaining there, the only thing is to see that you are there.

K: And you see that and discard it. Don't let us make a lot of fuss about it. As Balasundaram pointed out, the negative instantly becomes positive when I see. The false becomes the true instantly. The seeing is the rock; the hearing or listening is the rock.

The Centre and Duality

K: What is duality? Does duality exist at all?

A: Of course, it exists.

K: I won't postulate. I know nothing of Vedanta, Advaita, scientific theories. We are starting anew, not knowing the assumption of others, which may be second-hand. Wipe them all out. Is there duality? Apart from the factual duality—woman-man, light-darkness, tall-short—is there any other duality?

S: Duality of the 'I' and 'you' is structured within us.

K: Is there duality apart from the man-woman, dark-light: the obvious? I want to be clear that we are all talking of the same thing. I am not assuming that I am superior, I want to find out if there is duality, psychological duality. There is obvious duality outwardly—tall trees, short trees, different colours, different materials and so on. But psychologically, there is only 'what is' and because we are not able to solve 'what is', we invent the 'what should be'. So there is duality. From the fact, the 'what is', there is an abstraction to 'what should be', the ideal. But there is only 'what is'.

D: They say 'what is' is dualistic.

K: Wait, sir, I want to find out. I only know 'what is' and not 'what should be'.

P: 'What is' to me is duality.

K: No. But you are conditioned to duality, you are educated to duality, you function psychologically in duality.

S: The starting point is a dualistic position. It may be due to many factors.

K: That is what I want to investigate—whether this dualistic attitude towards life has come into being because the mind has not been able to solve actually 'what is'.

A: As far as we can see, the new-born baby does not cry only for mother's milk, for nourishment. It cries whenever it is left alone. Duality is the expression of an inadequacy in oneself for what I am. This begins almost from the beginning of life.

P: It is part of the racial heritage.

S: What is the nature of 'what is'?

K: That's what I want to get at. If I can understand 'what is', why should there be duality?

S: What is the instrument with which I understand?

B: Does the problem arise because there is no contact with 'what is'? Duality is postulated because there is very little contact with 'what is'.

K: That is what I want to find out. What is duality? Is duality a measurement?

B: Duality is a comparison.

P: Duality is the sense of 'I' as separate from the 'not-I'.

K: That is the basic cause of duality. Now, what is the 'I' that says you are different? What is the 'I'?

A: The centre, the body.

M: The brain.

P: I ask that question and in observing the movement of the 'I', I find that it is not something as factual as the chair or the table or the body. In itself it has no existence.

K: May I say something? It may sound absurd. There is no duality for me. There is woman-man, dark-light. We are not talking of that kind of duality. Duality exists only as the 'I' and the 'not-I', the space between the 'I' and the 'you', the centre as the 'I' and the centre as the 'you'. The centre of the 'I' looks at you and there is a distance between the 'I' and the 'you'. The distance can be expanded or narrowed down. This process is consciousness. Don't agree with me? I want to be clear, I want to start slowly.

B: This distance enclosed is consciousness.

M: Distance is in consciousness.

K: No, no, sir, there is distance between you and me sitting here, the physical distance. Then, there is the distance the mind has created which is the 'I' and the 'you'. The 'I' and the 'not-I', the 'you' and the distance is consciousness.

D: You should distinguish between the physical and the psychological.

S: Is the 'I' a concrete entity?

P: That's why I say this enquiry into who is the 'I' is difficult.

S: We started with what is duality—the 'I' and the 'not-I', the centre.

K: The space between this centre and that centre, the movement between this centre and that centre, the vertical, horizontal movement, is consciousness.

P: Is that all?

K: I am just beginning.

A: Sir, you have suggested two centres—this centre which comes across another centre. There is no other centre, sir.

K: I am coming to that. Go slowly, step by step. The other centre is invented by this centre.

A: I don't know. I say that even without the other centre, the distance comes.

S: Achyutji, the 'I' creates the 'not-I'. It is implied in the 'I' process.

118

K: If I have no centre, there is no other centre. I want to question the whole structure of duality. I don't accept it. You have accepted it. Our philosophy, our judgement, everything is based on this acceptance. The 'I' and the 'not-I' and all the complications arising out of it, and I want to, if I may, question the whole structure of duality. So, the 'I' is the only centre. From there, the 'not-I' arises and the relationship between the 'I' and the 'not-I' inevitably brings about conflict. There is only the centre from which arises the other centre, the 'you'. I think that is fairly clear; at least for me. Don't accept it.

M: How does this centre arise? Because I have this centre, I create the other centre.

K: I am coming to that. I don't want to answer that yet. In the waking state, the centre creates the other centre. In that, the whole problem of relationship arises, and therefore duality arises, the conflicts, the attempt to overcome duality. It is the centre that creates this division. I see that in the waking state because there is a centre, its relationship will always be divided. Division is space and time and where there is time and space as division, there must inevitably be conflict. That is simple, clear. So I see during the waking state, what is going on all the time is adjustment, comparison, violence, imitation. When the centre goes to sleep it maintains the division even when it sleeps.

SWS: What do you mean by saying the centre goes to sleep?

K: We don't know what that state is. We are going to investigate.

S: In waking consciousness the experiencer is the centre.

K: The experiencer is the centre, the centre is memory, the centre is knowledge, which is always in the past. The centre may project into the future but it still has its roots in the past.

D: The centre is the present, I don't know the past or the future.

K: You would never say that, if you have a centre.

D: So far as my identity is concerned, the past and the future are only accretions, I have nothing to do with them. I am the present.

A: You are the child of the past, you are the heir to everything of the past.

D: Not at all. That is an hypothesis. How do I know the past?

K: The language you are speaking in, English, is the result of the past.

P: If one exists, the other exists.

D: That is a theory.

A: How can that be a theory? The very fact that you come into existence implies that you are the child of the past.

D: I don't know the past, I don't know the future.

P: If one is free of both the past and the future, then there is no problem. Let us talk about people who are concerned with the past.

D: I am a very small non-entity with a feeling of 'I'-ness. I know nothing about the past or the future.

A: Is the 'I' not created and produced by the totality of the past—my father, my grandfather? How can I deny that? My consciousness itself is made up of the past.

P: There is the personal, racial, human past. Look, Deshpande, I remember the discussion of yesterday and the discussion comes in the way of my discussing today.

D: My position is, I don't know about the past or the future. It is an accretion.

A: Deshpandeji, when you say I am the present, please think. Do you mean to say that you are only this moment, with no past and no future? Is it a theory or a fact? Then you are in samadhi.

K: Just a minute, sir. Let us be quiet. You speak English. That is an accretion. What is the centre that accretes?

D: That centre I call 'I', but I don't know.

120

K: So the centre which has accumulated is the 'I'.

D: The accumulator and the accumulated are not the same.

K: Who is the centre that is accumulating? Is there a centre without accumulation? Is the centre different from the thing it has accumulated?

D: I can't answer that.

M: All that is the content of consciousness.

K: We said the content of consciousness is consciousness. If there is no consciousness, there is no accumulation.

M: I have not said that.

K: I have said it, we started with it.

M: The content of consciousness is consciousness. That means, when there is no content there is no consciousness.

K: That is what it means.

D: So it means that there is non-dual consciousness.

K: No, no. That is a speculation. Stick to what we started out with. Consciousness is its content. The content is consciousness. This is an absolute fact.

A: Sir, at any given time, this 'I' is not able to command the whole field of consciousness as its purview of perception. In my perception, I don't see the whole field.

K: Because there is a centre. Where there is a centre, there is fragmentation.

P: The 'I' is only operational through a process of thinking which is fragmentary.

K: That is all.

A: What I thought was that the content of consciousness has to be part of my field of perception. Is it not so?

P: If it were part of my perception, then the whole content of consciousness is consciousness and there is nothing else. Then I would rest with consciousness. I would remain there. But I sit in front of you and say, 'Show me the way,' and you keep on saying 'The moment you ask the way, you will never know the way.' We still ask you to show the way.

S: The first point is that we experience only fragmentarily and not total consciousness.

K: That is what I am saying. As long as there is a centre, there must be fragmentation and the fragmentation is the 'me' and the 'you' and the conflict in that relationship.

S: Are you equating this centre with consciousness or is it a fragment of total consciousness?

K: The centre is the content of consciousness.

S: So consciousness itself is fragmented?

P: You say this centre is time-space, you also seem to postulate the possibility of going beyond the field of time-space. The centre is that which operates. It is not able to go beyond. If it could, time and space would cease to be the content of consciousness.

K: Let us start again. The content of consciousness is consciousness. That is irrefutable. The centre is the maker of fragments. the centre becomes aware of the fragments when the fragments are agitated or in action; otherwise, the centre is not conscious of the other fragments. The centre is the observer of the fragments. The centre does not identify itself with the fragments. So there is always the observer and the observed, and the thinker and the experience. So, the centre is the maker of fragments and the centre tries to gather the fragments together and go beyond. One of the fragments says, 'sleep' and one of the fragments says 'keep awake'. In the state of keeping awake, there is disorder. The brain cells during sleep try to bring order because you cannot function effectively in disorder.

S: The brain tries to bring order. Is that process dualistic or non-dualistic?

K: I'll show it to you. The brain cells demand order. Otherwise, they cannot function. There is no duality in this. During the day, there is disorder because the centre is there, the centre is the cause of fragmentation; fragmentation it knows only through fragments; it is not conscious of the totality of fragments and, therefore, there is no order and, therefore, it lives in disorder. It is disorder. Though it says 'I must experience', it is living in disorder, living in confusion. It cannot do anything else but create disorder because it functions only in fragmentation. Right sir?

A: Yes, sir. It is so.

K: The brain cells need order; otherwise, they become neurotic, destructive. That is a fact. The brain cells are always demanding order and the centre is always creating fragmentation. The brain cells need order. This order is denied when there is a centre because the centre is always creating destruction, division, conflict and all the rest of it, which is a denial of security, which is denial of order. There is no duality. This process is going on. The brain saying 'I must have order', is not duality.

A: Are they two independent movements?

P: I feel we are moving away from the thing which is tangible to us.

K: This is very tangible.

P: It is not tangible. The brain cells seeking order is not tangible.

K: I will show it to you in a minute.

S: Pupulji, the whole physical world, in spite of chaos, maintains an extraordinary order. It is the very nature of the universe to maintain order.

P: The scientists' sense of time is not a real thing to us. The brain cells seeking order is not a real thing with us. I don't know but it may be. You are moving away from a fact to a fact which is beyond our comprehension.

K: P, we both see the point. Where there is a centre, there must be conflict, there must be fragmentation, there must be every form of division between the 'you' and the 'me', but the centre is creating this division. How do you know?

P: Because I have observed it in myself?

K: Verbally or factually?

P: Factually.

K: The centre is the maker of fragments. The centre is the fragment. This whole field is disorder. How are you aware of this disorder?

P: I have seen it.

K: Wait, you are not answering my question. Forgive me. I am asking you, How are you aware of this disorder? If it is the centre that is aware that it is disorder, then it is still disorder.

P: I see that.

K: You see that when the centre is aware that this is disorder then it creates a duality as order and disorder. So, how do you observe disorder—without the centre or with the centre? If it is an observation with the centre, there is a division. If there is no observation of the centre, then there is only disorder.

P: Or order.

K: Wait. Please go slowly. When the centre is aware that there is disorder, there is division, and this division is the very essence of disorder. When the centre is not there and aware, what takes place?

P: Then there is no centre; no disorder.

K: Therefore, what has taken place? There is no disorder. That is a fact. That is what the brain cells demand.

P: When you bring *that* in, you take *this* away. Let us now proceed.

K: Stop there. So I have discovered something, that the centre creates space and time. Where there is space and time, there must be division in relationship and, therefore, disorder in relationship. Having disorder in relationship, it creates further disorder because that is the very nature of the centre. There is not only disorder in relationship, there is disorder in thought, action, idea.

P: I want to ask you a question: Which is the fact—the perception of order or . . .?

K: You are only aware of disorder. Just listen. I am also feeling my way, you understand. I see the centre is the source of disorder wherever it moves—in relationship, in thought, in action, in perception. There is the perceiver and the perceived. So, wherever the centre operates, moves, functions, has its momentum, there must be division, conflict and all the rest of it. Where there is the centre, there is disorder. Disorder is the centre. How are you aware? Is the centre aware of the disorder or is there only disorder? If there is no centre to be aware of disorder, there is complete order. Then the fragments come to an end, obviously, because there is no centre which is making the fragments.

P: In that sense, the moment the fragments exist, the reality is the fragment. When the fragments end, the reality is non-fact. So, there is no division. You are back into the Vedantic position.

K: I refuse to accept it.

P: I am putting it to you.

A: I would say that when you say that 'I' is the source and the centre of disorder, or the centre is the source and it is disorder, that is a fact for me. When you say that if there is no centre observing that disorder——

K: No. I asked: Who is observing the disorder? Achyutji, see this. There is no consciousness of order. And that is the beauty of order.

125

P: What does the word 'reality' mean to you?

K: Nothing.

P: What do you mean by that? I would like to explore that word 'nothing'.

K: When it is something, it is not aware.

A: The field of cognition is the field of unreality.

K: No, be careful, sir. Just a minute. Leave that now. Let us go into the question of the dream because that is apparently one of the fragments of our life. What are dreams? What is the matrix of the structure of dreams? How do they happen?

Q: It happens when desires are not fulfilled during the day.

K: So, you are saying during the day I desire something and it has not been fulfilled, carried out, it has not been worked out. So, the desire continues.

P: Why do we go beyond? Thought is an endless process without a beginning, expelled from the brain cells. In the same way, there is a period when the mind is totally asleep; it is another form of the same propulsion.

K: It is exactly the same thing. The movement of the day still goes on. So, the centre which is the factor of disorder, creating disorder during the day, still goes on, the movement which becomes dreams, symbolic or otherwise, is the same movement.

M: You keep on saying that the centre is the source of disorder.

K: The centre is disorder, not the source.

M: The sense of 'I' is a constant demand longing for order. There is nobody to create it, and I am in this world begging for order, searching for order, and all the duality is a given duality, not a created duality.

K: No, sorry.

M: I find it is so. I don't want duality.

K: This search itself is duality. All our life is a search for non-duality.

M: I know that whatever I do is for the sake of order. The order may be temporary, a petty little order, but still there is no gesture, there is no posture of mind which does not aim at order, whether one is eating, drinking or sleeping. It also makes life possible. So, chaos is something which is imposed on me, disorder is forced on me. That is my observation. If you say it is not, then my observation and your observation differ.

P: In all observations, we have sat with Krishnaji and we have observed the self in operation and the nature of the self has been revealed.

M: No, it is only an hypothesis. We are playing with words. The mind is incapable of co-ordinating the factors. There is no such thing as a revelation in this, sir. There is nobody to tell us.

P: I agree. The very process of self-observation reveals it. It is not somebody telling you.

K: This man says this centre is the source of disorder. The movement of daily life continues in sleep. It is the same movement and dreams are the expression of that 'me'. When I wake up, I say 'I have had dreams'. That is only a means of communication; dreams are 'me', dreams are not separate from the centre which has created this movement, this disorder. The next factor is deep sleep. Are you aware when you are deeply asleep?

S: Who is aware that there has been deep sleep? One is not conscious of deep sleep. You don't say: 'I have had an extraordinary sleep.' You may say: 'I have had no dreams, I had a peaceful sleep.'

P: It is really saying that you have had a good sleep.

M: When I am deeply asleep, I am fully aware that I have no thoughts, I have no consciousness.

K: So, all that one can say is: 'I have had a very good sleep without

127

dreams.' How does one investigate that state which is without dreams, a state which you called just now deep sleep? Do you do it through the conscious mind or a theory, or by repeating what somebody has said about it? How do you go into it?

S: The sleep has to reveal itself. Otherwise, you cannot go into the other state.

K: Why do you want to go into it?

S: Because I want to know whether it is the same state.

P: There is a state of being 'awake' and a state of 'deep sleep'.

SWS: My own experience is that when there is a sleep without dream, there is no centre. Then the centre comes again, it remembers that I have slept without dreams, again the centre starts its operation.

S: Deep sleep is a sleep without a centre.

K: Why don't we only talk about what is knowable?

P: But you wanted to investigate deep sleep. Is it possible to investigate deep sleep?

D: I see only one fact: in sleep there is no centre.

K: That gentleman said deep sleep means no centre.

M: Deep sleep means very low intensity of consciousness.

P: I asked the question: Is it possible to investigate into deep sleep?

K: What do you mean by 'investigate'? Can I investigate, can the centre investigate? You watch the film at the cinema. You are not identifying with it; you are not part of it; you are merely observing.

S: What is it that is observing without identifying?

K: There is no one to observe. There is only observation.

S: What Pupul is asking is: Can deep sleep be investigated?

128

K: We understand that. Can it be revealed, can it be exposed, can it be observable? I say 'yes'. Can I observe you, just observe without naming? Of course, it is possible. The observer is the centre, the observer is the past, the observer is the divider; the observer is the space between you and me.

P: First of all, you should have the tools, the instruments with which this is possible. One has to have a state of awareness where this is possible. It is only when there is this state of awareness or *jagriti*, that it is possible.

K: Is there an obsevation of this disorder without the centre becoming aware that there is disorder? If that can be solved, I have solved the whole momentum of it. What is order? We said the centre can never be aware of order. Then, what is that state? Then, what is virtue of which there is no consciousness of being virtuous? What man traditionally accepts as virtue is practice. Vanity practising humility is still vanity. Then, what is virtue? It is a state in which there is no consciousness of being virtuous. I am just exploring. If the centre is aware that it has humility, it is not humility. Virtue is a state of mind where it is not conscious that it is virtuous. Therefore, it topples all the practices, all the sadhanas. To see disorder not from a centre is order. That order you cannot be conscious of. If you are conscious of it, it is disorder.

The Nature of Despair

P: Can we examine the roots of despair? It is a very real problem in our life. In a sense, the root of sorrow is the root of despair; it must be of the same nature.

K: I wonder what is despair. I have never felt it. Therefore, please convey it to me. What do you mean by 'despair'?

P: A sense of utter futility.

K: Is that it—a sense of utter futility? I doubt that. It is not quite that. Not knowing what to do, would you call that despair?

R: The total absence of meaning and significance: is that what you mean?

FW: I would like to suggest 'a state of paralysed hope'.

P: Despair, in a sense, has really nothing to do with hope.

K: Is it related to sorrow? Is it self-pity? I am questioning, I am not suggesting.

P: It is not self-pity. Self-pity is narrow in its dimension.

K: We are investigating. Is it related to sorrow? Is sorrow related to despair and the sense of deep self-pity that can't find a way out?

P: I feel all these descriptions are narrow.

K: They are narrow, but we will make them wider. Would you say it is the end of the road, reaching the end of the tether? If there is no way around something, you look somewhere else, but that doesn't mean despair.

FW: I could imagine that the mother whose child dies is desperate.

K: Not quite. I won't call that desperate. I should think this is related to sorrow.

P: Have we not all known despair?

K: I don't know. I am asking; tell me.

P: There is an utter and total sense of futility.

K: No, Pupul. Instead of 'futility' use a more significant word—futility is so futile—put it another way.

R: I think it is the end of the tether.

K: End of hope, end of search, end of relationship. Does somebody else know despair?

FW: I think it is a blank wall.

K: Blank wall is not despair.

A: Something dies even before your body has died.

K: Is that despair?

Par: Utter helplessness.

B: Is there any relationship to sorrow? I think it is the bottom of sorrow, the pit of sorrow.

K: Balasundaram, you mean to say you have never known despair?

Par: It is the opposite of hope.

K: No, Doctor. Do you know what despair is? Could you tell me what it is?

Par: A state resulting from failures.

K: Failure? You are making it much too small. I think despair has rather a large canvas. I have talked to people who were in despair. Apparently, none of you know despair. Do you?

R: I don't think I know despair. I know what suffering is.

K: I want to question. When we talk about despair, is it something profound, or is it merely the end of one's tether?

P: You know despair. Now, tell us a little about it.

Par: Is it darkness?

K: No, sir. Do you know what despair is? A man who is suffering knows exactly what it means. He doesn't beat about the bush. He says I have suffered, I know my son is dead, and there is an appalling sense of isolation, loss, a sense of self-pity, a tremendous storm; it is a crisis. Would you say despair is a crisis?

JC: Yes, sir.

K: Don't please agree with me yet. Apparently, except for one or two, nobody seems to be in despair.

R: Is it a form of escape from suffering?

K: In despair, is jealousy involved, a sense of loss? I possess you and you suddenly drop me, build a wall against me—is that part of despair? I am sorry this is something quite out of my depth. I am not saying it is valid or not valid; but I am just asking what is 'despair'? What is the dictionary meaning?

FW: The root of the word comes from hope.

K: Have you been in despair, sir? Using the common word, which you and I use, do you know what it means—despair? Is it a deep sense of fear?

P: When you get to the depths of yourself, to the very root of yourself, do you think it is possible to distinguish between fear and despair?

K: No, then why do you use the word 'despair'?

A: Sir, I think the word despair is distinct from the sense of fear.

P: When you hit the bottom, then it is very difficult to differentiate between fear, sorrow, despair.

K: May I ask—not you personally—have you really reached the lowest depths of yourself? And when you do, is it despair?

P: Sir, when you ask that question, there can be no possible answer. How does one know the depths?

K: Is it a sense of helplessness or is it much more than that?

P: It is much more than that. Because in helplessness you have hope.

K: Therefore, it is something much more significant than hope. What is that feeling or what is that state where one feels completely, utterly in despair? Is it that no movement of any kind takes place, and since there is no movement, would you call that despair?

P: How do you differentiate?

K: Look, I love my son and he has gone to the dogs and I can't do anything. I can't even talk to him, I can't even approach him, I can't go near him, touch him. Would that state be despair? The word 'desperate': desperate and despair. Would you consider to be desperate a state of despair?

FW: We sometimes say: 'I desperately want something.' There is a projection in it that I want something.

P: There is an urgency towards a direction in that. There is no urgency towards anything in this.

FW: Then despair is not the proper word.

P: Despair is a very important word in living.

B: It is also lack of energy. To be in despair is not to be desperate for something—but to touch the nadir of energy they are all one.

P: When you plunge into depths, you cannot separate sorrow from despair. I do not think that the distinction is fundamentally valid.

S: Pupulji, when you started, you wanted to make a distinction between despair and sorrow.

P: I am finding that when you go down, delve, the distinction between despair and sorrow does not exist.

K: Are you asking what is the root of sorrow?

P: No, sir. I find that it is not possible for me to divide sorrow from despair.

JC: Despair is a feeling of nothingness.

FW: But the root of the word must have some significance.

P: It may have no significance. A word may not cover its meaning. Sir, some people must have come to you in despair. There is the sorrow of nothingness, of despair.

K: Pupulji, are we saying despair is related to sorrow, related to that sense of total abnegation of all relationship?

P: Yes, a total anguish.

K: A total anguish, the total feeling of complete isolation which means having no access or no relationship to anything. Is despair related to sorrow, related to isolation, withholding?

JC: There is a finality to it, the end of all your hope or your expectation.

K: Have you, or anyone reached that point? The darkness of the soul, the Christians call it, the dark night of the soul? Would you call it that? Is that despair? That is much more potent than despair.

P: You can't tell me that I am at this level or that level.

K: May we begin this way, Pupul? Let us use the word and the depth of that word, the meaning of that word 'sorrow' first. Begin with that.

P: In varying degrees, we all know sorrow.

K: Grief, a sense of helplessness, a sense of no way out. Does that bring about despair?

P: That is despair. Why do you object?

134

K: I would not call it despair. Let us go slowly. Let us feel our way. My son is dead, and that is what I call sorrow. I have lost him. I will never see him again. I lived with him, we had played together, everything is gone and suddenly overnight I realize how utterly lonely I am. Would you call that feeling, that deep sense of loneliness, not having a companion, despair? Or, is it that sense of deep awareness, of a total lack of any kind of relationship with anybody, which is loneliness? Would you say that loneliness is despair?

P: You use a word to describe a situation, to fit a situation.

K: I will describe the situation.

P: You can use the word 'sorrow' or you can use 'despair' but the situation remains the same.

K: What is it, how to get out of it, what to do with it?

P: No, you have said 'remain totally with sorrow'. Is sorrow the summation of all energy?

K: I don't follow.

P: You have said that in the depth of sorrow is the summation of all energy. This must be of the same nature.

K: I understand what you are saying. Last night K said sorrow is the essence of all energy, the quintessence of all energy. All energy is focused there; I think that's right. Now, is that a fact? Is that an actuality?

P: This morning, I certainly had a feeling of the other which I call despair. I certainly had it, total, absolute. Whatever statement I make now, will move me away.

K: Look, Pupul, I think I am getting it. My son is dead and I realize what is involved in that. That is a fact which can never be altered. Is the refusal to accept the actual fact despair? I totally, completely, accept that my son is dead. I can't do anything about it. He is gone. I remain with the fact. I don't call that despair, sorrow, I don't give it a name. I remain with the actual fact that he

135

is finished. What do you say? Can you remain with that fact without any movement away from it?

P: Is the sorrow or despair also not an unalterable fact?

K: No . . . Let us look at it slowly, carefully. I loved my son and suddenly he is gone. The result of that is, there is a tremendous sense of energy which is translated as sorrow. Right? The word 'sorrow' indicates this fact; only that fact remains. That is not despair.

Let us move away from that. I want to see what actually takes place when there is this enormous crisis and the mind realizes that any form of escape is a projection into the future, and remains with that fact without any movement. The fact is immovable. Can I remain, can the mind remain with that immovable fact and not move away from it? Let us make it very very simple. I am angry, furious because I have given my life to something and I find somebody has betrayed that, and I feel furious. That fury is all energy. You follow? I haven't acted upon that energy. It is a gathering of all your energy which is expressed in a fury of anger. Can I remain with that fury of anger? Not translate, not hit out, not rationalize, just hold it. Is it possible? What happens? I won't even call it despair.

A: Would you say it is a state of depression?

K: No, no. That is reaction. This I remain with. It is going to tell me. I am not going to call it depression. That means I am acting upon it.

A: I am saying that the patient is there, there is an infection and a fever. Now the fever is the symptom of that infection. In that way I have watched myself with anger without trying to do anything to it.

K: No, Achyutji, I don't mean that you watch it. You *are* that anger, you *are* that total fury and that total energy of that fury.

A: There is no energy. What goes with it is a feeling of total helplessness.

K: No, sir. I think I understand what Pupulji is talking about, which is, I have come to realize that I am caught in a net of my own making, and I can't move, I am paralysed. Would that be despair?

JC: If a woman who can't swim sees her son drowning in the sea, then I think there is absolute despair, because she knows that he could be saved, but she is unable to do it. You follow?

K: Very well, sir. But I think we are getting away from something. We are now describing in different ways the meaning of despair, the meaning of sorrow, the meaning of all that.

A: The condition that you have described just now and what Pupulji was describing is different from anger. Anger is the reaction to somebody's else's behaviour. This is a reaction to your own situation.

K: It is not a reaction, but an awareness of one's own insufficiency and that insufficiency at its depth, not superficially, is despair, is that it?

FW: Isn't there much more than this? I question this awareness of insufficiency, because there is already the element of not wanting to accept that insufficiency.

P: How do you know?

FW: I have tried to gather from what you said.

K: Look, Fritz, either you feel it or it is not a fact. Would you say, if I may ask, have you ever felt totally insufficient?

FW: I can't remember. I don't know.

K: But I come to you and I say I have felt this total insufficiency and I want to understand it, it is boiling in me, I am in a desperate state about it. How would you tackle it? How would you help me go beyond it?

FW: I know something quite similar to that, for example most of the things in life I am unable to understand and I also see that my brain is completely inadequate to understand. So, if you mean that insufficiency, I am aware of that insufficiency.

K: Sir, I realize I am insufficient. I am aware of it. Then I try to fill it with various things. I know I am filling it and I see as I fill it, it is still empty, still insufficient. I have come to the point when I see that whatever I do, that insufficiency can never be wiped out; filled. That is real sorrow or despair. Is that it, Pupulji? Look, I want to get at something here. May I proceed? My son is dead. I am not only desperate, but I am in profound shock, profound sense of loss which I call sorrow. My instinctual response is to run away, is to explain, is to act upon it. Now, I realize the futility of that and I don't act. I won't call it sorrow, I won't call it despair, I won't call it anger, but I see the fact is the only thing; nothing else. Everything else is non-fact. Now, what takes place there? That's what I want to get at. If that is despair, if you remain with it without naming it, without recognizing it, if you remain with it totally without any movement of thought, what takes place? That's what we are going to discuss.

R: It is very difficult because thought says remain with it, and that is still thought.

K: No, that's an intellectual game. That is totally invalid. I meet an immovable fact and come to it with a desperate desire to move it, for whatever reason—love, affection, whatever motive, and so I battle against it, but the fact cannot be changed. Can I face the fact without any sense of hope, despair, all that verbal structure and just say, 'Yes, I am what I am'? I think then some kind of explosive action takes place if I can remain there.

A: Sir, there is some purgation called for, before this happens. Some purgation of the heart is called for, as I see it.

K: I won't call it purgation. See, Achyutji, you know what sorrow is, don't you? Can you remain with it without any movement? What takes place when there is no movement? I am getting it now—when my son is dead, that is an immovable irrevocable fact; and when I remain with it, which is also an immovable, irreconcilable fact, the two facts meet.

138

P: In the profundity of sorrow without any known cause, there is nothing to react to, there is no incident to react to.

K: No analytical process is possible, I understand.

P: In a sense thought is paralysed there.

K: Yes, that's it. There is the immovable fact that my son is dead and also that I have no escape is another fact. So, when these two facts meet, what takes place?

P: As I said, the past is still there not because of any volition.

K: I understand.

P: Now, what is possible after that?

JC: Our lack of awareness will not allow two facts.

K: That's what I want to find out. Something must happen. I am questioning whether there are two facts or only one fact. The fact that my son is dead and the fact that I must not move away from it. The latter is not a fact. That is an idea, and therefore it is not a fact. There is only one fact. My son is dead. That is an absolute, immovable fact. It is an actuality. And I say to myself, I must not escape, I must meet it completely. And I say that is fact. I question if it is a fact. It is an idea. It is not a fact as is the fact that my son is dead. He is gone. There is only one fact. When you separate the fact from yourself and say, 'I must meet it with all my attention,' that's non-fact. The fact is the other.

S: But my movement is a fact. Isn't it?

K: Is it a fact or is it an idea?

S: Not wanting to stay there, but moving away from that energy of anger or moving away from the energy of hurt, isn't it a fact?

K: Yes, of course. You remember, we discussed the other day—an abstraction can be a fact. I believe I am Jesus. That is a fact, as is the fact that I believe 'I am a good man'. Both are facts; both are brought about by thought. That's all. Sorrow is not brought about

139

by thought, but by an actuality which has been translated as sorrow.

S: Sorrow is not brought about by thought?

K: Wait, wait, go into it slowly. I am not sure. As I said, this is a dialogue, discussion. I say something. You must tear it up.

S: There are different types of sorrow.

K: No, no. My son is dead, that is a fact.

R: And the question is of meeting the fact that he is not there.

JC: Sorrow is not a fact?

K: My son is dead. That is a fact. And that fact reveals the nature of my relationship to him, my commitment to him, my attachment to him, etc. which are all non-facts.

P: Sir, that comes later. When my son dies, there is only one thing.

K: That's all I am saying.

P: Actually if your son is dead, in that moment can the mind move away?

K: For the moment it is paralysed, totally paralysed.

P: That is the moment.

K: No, look, my son is dead, and I am paralysed by it; both psychologically and physiologically I am in a state of shock. That shock wears off.

P: In a sense, the intensity of that state has already dissipated itself.

K: No. Shock is not a realization of the fact. It is a physical shock. Somebody has hit me on the head.

P: There is shock.

K: That's all. Paralysis has taken place, for a few days, for a few hours, few minutes. When a shock takes place, my consciousness is not functioning.

140

P: Something is functioning.

K: No, just tears. It is paralysed. That is one state. But it is not a permanent state. It is a transient state out of which I am going to emerge.

P: But the moment I start coming out . . .

K: No, the shock I got, there I face reality.

P: How do you face reality?

K: Let us see. My brother or sister dies, and at the moment, that moment may last a few days or a few hours, it is a tremendous psychosomatic shock. There is no activity of the mind, no activity of consciousness. This is like being paralysed. That is not a state.

P: It is sorrow, that is the energy of sorrow.

K: That energy has been much too strong.

P: Any movement away dissipates that energy?

K: No, but the body cannot remain psychosomatically in a state of shock.

P: Then, how does it face sorrow?

K: I am coming to that. It is like a man who is paralysed and wanting to speak. He can't.

P: What takes place when shock goes?

K: You are waking up to the fact, the fact that your son is dead. Thought then begins, the whole movement of thought begins. There are tears. I say, 'I wish I had behaved properly, I wish I had not said those last cruel words at the last minute.' Then, you begin to escape from that—'I would like to meet my brother in my next life, in the astral place.' I escape. I am saying if you don't escape and don't observe the fact as though different from yourself, then the observer is the observed.

P: The whole of that thing is that initial state of shock.

141

K: I question that, Pupul. Go into it a bit more. It is a shock which the body and the psyche cannot tolerate, there is paralysis which has taken place.

P: But if there is energy?

K: It is too strong. It is much too strong. This is a fact.

P: Let us go slowly, sir.

K: Then, we are not talking about the same thing.

P: It is at the instant of death that there is a total realization of this. It then gets dissipated.

K: No, would you put it this way, Pupul? Leave aside death for the moment.

P: But that is also a total thing.

K: Wait, I am coming to that. When there is death, the tremendous shock has driven out everything. It is not the same as the mountain, that marvellous scenery. These two are entirely different.

P: It depends, sir, on the state of the mind.

K: It depends on the state of relationship.

P: And the state of mind when death actually takes place.

K: Yes. So what are we discussing? What are we having a dialogue about?

P: We are trying to discover how in this maximum energy-quotient which arises out of despair, death, sorrow; what is the chemical alchemy which transforms the energy which is seemingly destructive and hurtful into what you call passion. If one allows sorrow or despair to corrode one, which is a natural process, then you have brought in another element.

K: When energy is not dissipated through words, when the energy of the shock of some great event is not dissipated, that energy without a motive has quite a different significance.

142

P: If I may ask, this holding it in consciousness . . .

K: It is not in consciousness.

P: Is it not in consciousness?

K: It is not in consciousness. If you hold it in your consciousness, it is part of thought. Your consciousness is put together by thought.

S: It has arisen in consciousness.

K: No.

S: Then, what is it?

K: The holding of it, not running away from it, remaining with it.

P: What is the entity that does not move?

K: There is no entity.

P: Then what is it?

K: The entity is when there is movement away from the fact.

P: How does the entity end itself?

K: Look, Pupul, let us make it very simple, clear.

P: It is very important.

K: I agree, it is very interesting. There is a shock. The realization is gone out of the shock, there is sorrow. The very word 'sorrow' is a distraction. The escape is a distraction away from the fact. To remain totally with that fact means no interference of the movement of thought; therefore, you are now not consciously holding it. I will repeat it. Consciousness is put together by thought. Content makes thought. The event of my son's death is not thought, but when I bring it into thought, it is within my consciousness. That is very important. I have discovered something.

P: Is the very force of that energy that which totally silences thought?

K: Put it that way if you like. Thought cannot touch it. But our conditioning, our tradition, our education is to touch it, change, modify, rationalize, run away from it, which is the activity of consciousness.

R: The crux of it seems to be giving a name to the form that it takes and that is the seed from which the rest of the distraction grows.

K: It is very interesting. I can't remember when my brother died. But from what Shivarao and others have told me, it seems that there was a shock period, and when K came out of it, he remained with that thing; he did not go to Dr Besant and ask for help. So, now I can see how it happens. The shock; when the shock is over, you come to the fact that a tremendous event has taken place—death; not mine or yours, my brother's or your brother's, but death has taken place, which is an extraordinary event as is birth. Now, can one look at it, observe it without consciousness as thought entering into it?

P: Let us go back to sorrow. You have said: 'Sorrow is not born of thought.'

K: Yes. Sorrow is not born of thought. What do you say about it?

P: When the death of sorrow is, thought is not.

K: Wait, wait, Pupul. Sorrow is not the child of thought. That's what K said. Why? The word 'sorrow' is thought. The word is not the thing, therefore that feeling of sorrow is not the word. When the word is used, it becomes thought.

JC: We are talking about a situation where there has been a shock. The access of that energy, the return to consciousness is sorrow.

K: I have named it as sorrow.

JC: That is the return to the state of sorrow.

K: No. There is shock. Then, there is the moving away from that shock.

P: If sorrow is stripped of the word . . .

K: Of course. That's why I want to be very clear. The word is not

144

the thing, therefore that feeling of sorrow is not the word. If the word is not, thought is not.

P: Sorrow is one thing; even if you remove the word, the content is.

K: Of course. So, is it possible not to name it? The moment you name it, you bring it into consciousness.

S: Prior to naming, is the existing condition not part of consciousness? The word is 'sorrow': the moment you name it as 'sorrow', that is a different thing. The 'what is' which is not named, is it part of consciousness?

K: We said consciousness is its content. Its content is put together by thought. An incident takes place where the energy shock drives out consciousness for a second or for days or months or whatever it is. Then, as the shock wears off, you begin to name the state. Then, you bring that into consciousness. But it is not in consciousness when it takes place.

Registration, the Movement of Millennia

P: Krishnaji, you have spoken about holding the quality of anger, fear or any strong emotion, without the word, in consciousness. Could we probe into that? The wiping away, whether it is a hurt, fear, anger or any one of the darknesses within one, is only possible if what you are talking about takes place. Can we come to that passion of feeling, which goes behind all these words of fear, anger, etc.? Can that be held in consciousness?

K: What does it mean to hold the feeling of anger, whatever 'is', without the word? Is this possible?

P: And is there anything without the word?

K: Go on.

FW: Is there fear when there is not the word 'fear'? And what is the nature of the energy in the body or in the whole being if there is no naming?

A: Clarity for us means naming. When we want to probe into a strong feeling, a disturbance, we want to know precisely what it is, we don't want any self-deception. Invariably, before we have been able to grasp it completely, we have named it. So, naming is both our instrument of clarity and the cause of confusion.

K: Is the word different from the fact, from 'what is'? Is the word 'door' different from the door? The word 'door' is not the actuality. So, the word is not the thing.

S: The question arises, then, can one ever indicate the actuality?

K: We are going to find out. We are going into it slowly.

R: Is there a difference between the statements, 'the word "door"'

146

is not the door' and ' "Fear" is not fear'? The two things seem to be different.

K: The word 'door' is not the actuality. The name 'K' is not the actuality; the form is not the actuality. So, the word is not the thing. The 'door', the word, is different from the actuality. We are trying to find out if the word 'fear' is different from the actuality. Does the actuality represent the word and without the word is there the actuality?

S: What is the feeling of fear without the word?

K: Let us go very very slowly. I want to make this perfectly clear to myself. There is the word 'fear', now is the word 'fear' different from the actuality, the emotion, the feeling of fear and without the word is there that feeling?

R: Word is thought.

K: So, the word is the medium through which thought expresses itself. Without the word, can thought express itself? Of course it can; a gesture, a look, a nod of the head, and so on. Without the word, thought can express itself to a very very limited extent. When you want to express something very complicated in thought, the word is necessary. But the word is not the actual thought, the actual state.

A: I raise one difficulty: we perceive with the senses. That process ends when there is naming. That starts the tertiary process. With the naming, a number of complicated things begin in my brain. Now, I see this and wipe out the word, the name. When I have wiped out the name, I have not wiped out the feeling.

K: I am not quite sure, Achyutji. Pupulji is asking, what is the quality of the mind that without the word can hold that feeling, without any movement, right?

R: But we are questioning whether the feeling arises without the word?

K: That is all.

147

P: If I may say so, there are many things in consciousness which arise prior to the word.

Rad: Primordial fear; but can it be sustained without the word?

P: I am not talking about sustaining. But there are various things, tenderness, joy for instance.

K: Can you observe something without the word? Can you observe me, the form, for the moment without the word?

P: Yes.

K: You can. Now, you are already observing the form, you have removed the word 'K' and you are observing the form.

P: We are observing. I don't say we are observing the form.

K: Then, what are you observing?

P: You see, sir, the moment you say 'I am observing the form', there has to be naming.

K: There has to be a name.

P: There has to be naming.

K: No.

P: Please listen, sir, when I say there is just observing, then the form is part of the whole observing field. I am observing, not only you, I am observing.

K: I said, remove the word 'K', and observe the form. That is all. Of course, you are observing. I am limiting it to just the form. Are you observing the form?

P: Yes. I am observing the form.

K: What are you trying to get at?

P: I am trying to see whether the word is prior to that.

K: Pupul, let us keep simple. There is fear. I want to find out whether the word has created that fear. The word is the recogni-

148

tion of that thing which I have called fear, because that fear has gone on for many years, and I have recognized it through the word. Ten years ago I was afraid, that fear is registered in my brain with the word. With the word is associated fear. It occurs again today and immediately the recognizing process sets in, which is the word, and so on. So, the word gives me a feeling that I have had before. The word encourages the feeling, has stabilized the feeling.

R: Yes. Sustains it.

K: It hold it. The word holds the thing by recognizing it, by remembering it and so on. Now, I am asking whether without the word there can be fear. The word is a process of recognition. Fritz, look at it. You are afraid. How do you know you are afraid?

FW: By naming it.

K: Now, how do you know it?

FW: I have been afraid before, so I know that feeling. So, as it comes again, I recognize it.

K: If you recognize it, it is a verbal process; if you don't recognize it, what is the state?

FW: There is no fear. There is energy in the body.

K: No, sir. Don't use the word 'energy' because we will go into something else. There is fear. I have recognized it by naming it. In naming it, I have put it into a catetgory and the brain remembers it, registers it, holds it. If there is no recognition, no verbal movement, would there be fear?

P: There is disturbance.

K: I am using the word 'fear'. Stick to fear.

P: If I may say so, fear is not such a simple thing that you can say, if there is no naming of it, fear is not . . .

K: I don't say that, yet. Of course, there is a lot of complexity involved in it.

149

P: It is a tremendous thing.

S: Psychologically, something happens even before naming takes place.

P: There are profoundly deep fears.

S: If we accept only this position that the word creates fear, that means there is no content to fear at all.

K: I don't say that. There is a process of recognition. If that process of recognition didn't exist, if that is at all possible, then, what is fear? I am not saying it doesn't exist. I am asking a question. If there is no process of registration, recording, which is memory in operation, what is the thing called fear?

P: Remove the word 'fear', and see what remains. Any word I use is going to apply exactly as much as the word 'fear'.

K: I am attacking it quite differently. You insult me because I have an image. There is an immediate registration taking place. I am asking: Can that registration come to an end when you insult me and so there is no recording at all?

S: I don't understand this. That is a totally different process.

K: It is exactly the same thing. Fear arises because I am afraid of the past. The past is registered and that incident in the past awakens the sense of fear. That fear has been registered. Is it possible to observe the new feeling, whatever it is, without bringing the past into action? Have you got it?

Rad: There is a feeling of recognition before you actually call it fear.

K: No, look. Let us go calmly. You insult me. I insult you. What takes place? You register it, don't you?

Rad: I register it when I recognize it initially. That itself creates a momentum.

K: Therefore, stop that momentum. Can that momentum be stopped? Look Radhika, let us put it much more simply. You are hurt. Aren't you? You are hurt from childhood for various reasons and it has been deeply registered in the mind, in the brain. The instinctive reaction is not to be hurt any more. So, you build a wall, withdraw. Now, without building the wall, can you know that you are hurt, can you be aware of it and the next time a process of hurt begins, not register it?

FW: What do you mean by registering?

K: Our brain is a tape recorder. It is registering all the time, there is like and dislike, pleasure and pain. It is moving, moving. I say something ugly to you and the brain immediately takes charge, registers it. Now, I say: 'Can you stop that registration, though it has registered? And next time if there is any insult, do not register it at all.' You understand what I am talking about? First, see the question. Is the question clear?

FW: That means not to form any image of it right away.

K: No, no. Just don't introduce the image for the moment. That becomes yet more complex. Can you recognize the word but not register it? I want to keep it very very simple. First, see this. The brain is registering all the time. You call me a fool, that is registered for various reasons. That is a fact. The next question is: Can that registration stop? Otherwise the mind, the brain, has no sense of freedom.

P: The brain is a live thing. It has to register. Registration is one thing, but the cutting of the momentum is the movement away from registration.

K: That is what I am talking about.

S: Aren't you speaking of two things: one is the stopping of the momentum and the other stopping registration altogether.

K: First, get what I am talking about. Then you can question. Then you can make it clear.

P: When you say do not register, does that mean the brain cells come to a stop?

K: Look, Pupulji, it is very important because if there is no possibility of stopping registration, then the brain becomes mechanical.

A: I want to question this, because you are over-simplifying the matter. Actually, our state of receiving anything is without our knowing that there is either a preference or an aversion, and fear is in that cycle. It arises from the past, and is not directly related to what I perceive. But it is that which perceives.

K: As long as the brain is registering all the time, it is moving from knowledge to knowledge. Now, I am challenging the word. I see knowledge is limited, fragmented and so on and I am asking myself whether registration can stop.

GM: Can the brain answer that question?

K: I think it can, in the sense the brain can become aware of its own registering process.

P: There are certain fears which you can deal with in that way. But fear has been the cry of man for millennia. And you are that cry.

K: I know. Stop. That cry of millennia is fear. The brain has been registering for millennia. Therefore, registering has become part of it. The brain has become mechanical. I say: Can that mechanical process stop? That is all. If it cannot be stopped it becomes merely a machine, which it is. This is all part of tradition, part of repetition, part of the constant registration through millennia. I am asking a simple question which has great depth to it, which is: Can it stop? If it cannot stop, man is never free.

Par: May I ask you a question? Why do we register at all?

K: For safety, security, protection, certainty. The registration is to give the brain a certain sense of security.

P: Isn't the brain itself involved? It has evolved through registration.

K: It has evolved through knowledge, which is registration.

P: What is it from within itself which says 'stop'?

K: Somebody challenges me.

P: What is the factor which makes you say 'stop'?

K: Someone comes along and says: Look, through millennia man has evolved through knowledge and at present you are certainly different from the great apes. And he says: Look, as long as you are registering, you are living a fragmentary life because knowledge is fragmentary and whatever you do from that fragmentary state of brain is incomplete. Therefore, there is pain, suffering. So, we are asking at the end of that explanation, can that registration, can that movement of the past, end? Listen. I am making it simple. Can this movement of millennia stop?

P: I am asking you this question: Is there something in the very quality of listening?

K: Yes, there is. That's it.

P: And that listening ends, silences this registration.

K: That is it. That is my point. You have come into my life by chance. You have come into my life and you have pointed out to me that my brain has evolved through knowledge, through registration, through experience; and that knowledge, that experience is fundamentally limited. And whatever action takes place from that limited state will be fragmentary and therefore there will be conflict, pain. Find out if that momentum which has tremendous volume, depth, can end. You know it is a tremendous flow of energy which is knowledge. Stop that knowledge. That is all.

FW: May I ask you a question? Much reference has been made to the tape-recorder which just goes on registering, and it can't stop itself. It has to be stopped. But then, can the brain stop itself?

K: We are going to find out. First, face the question, that is my point. First, listen to the question.

S: Is the whole of my consciousness only registration? In the whole of my consciousness, is there only registration going on?

153

K: Of course.

S: Then, what is it that can observe that registering?

K: What is it that can observe this registering or can prevent registering? I also know silence—the silence that is between two noises . . .

S: Is the silence which I experience also registered?

K: Obviously.

S: You can't use the word 'registering' for silence.

K: As long as there is this registration process going on, it is mechanical. Is there silence which is non-mechanistic? A silence which has not been thought about, induced, brought about or invented. Otherwise, the silence is merely mechanistic.

S: But one knows the non-mechanistic silence sometimes.

K: Not sometimes.

Raj: Sir, is it possible for a non-mechanistic silence to come?

K: No, no. I am not interested in that. I am asking something entirely different: this momentum, this conditioning, the whole of consciousness is the past. It is moving. There is no future consciousness. The whole consciousness is the past, registered, remembered, stored up as experience, knowledge, fear, pleasure. That is the whole momentum of the past. And somebody comes along and says: Listen to what I have to say, can you end that momentum? Otherwise this momentum, with its fragmentary activity, will go on endlessly.

Raj: I think this movement can be stopped only if you don't hang on to it.

K: No, the momentum is you. You are not different from the momentum. You don't recognize that you are this vast momentum, this river of tradition, of racial prejudices, the collective drive, the so-called individual assertions. If there is no stopping that, there is no future. So, there is no future if this current is going on.

154

You may call it a future, but it is only the same thing modified. There is no future. I wonder if you see this.

P: An action takes place and darkness arises in me. The question arises: Can consciousness with its own content, which is darkness——

K: End. Hold it.

P: What do you mean exactly?

K: Can you hold, can the brain hold this momentum, or is it an idea that it is momentum? You follow what I mean? Listen to it carefully. Is the momentum actual or is it an idea? If it is an idea, then you can hold the idea about the momentum. But, if it is not an idea, a conclusion, then the brain is directly in contact with the momentum. I wonder if you follow. And therefore, it can say: 'All right, I will watch.' It is watching, it is not allowing it to move. Now, is it the word you are holding on to, or are you observing this vast movement? Look, you are the vast movement. When you say you are that vast movement, is it an idea?

Raj: No.

K: Therefore, you are that. Find out if that thing can end—the past coming, meeting the present, a challenge, a question and ending there. Otherwise, there is no end to suffering. Man has put up with suffering for thousands upon thousands of years. That momentum is going on and on. I can give ten explanations—reincarnation, karma—but I still suffer. This suffering is the vast momentum of man. Can that momentum come to an end without control? The controller is the controlled. Can that momentum stop? If it does not stop, then there is no freedom, then action will always be incomplete. Can you see the whole of that, see it actually?

P: Can we ever see that? When we see feeling in the present, what is it we are seeing?

K: I call you a fool. Must you register it?

P: I can't just answer why should I register.

155

K: Don't register.

P: It is a question of whether these eyes and ears of mine are flowing out to the word; if they are still and listen, there is no registration. There is listening but no registration.

K: So, what are you seeing?

P: There is no seeing of this movement. I have been observing while this discussion has been going on and I say: What does it mean to register the fact? I am listening, you are listening. Obviously, if my listening is directed to the word, which is coming out of me, I register, and this very movement outward throws it back. But if the eyes and the ears are seeing and listening, but still, then they take in without any registration.

K: So, you are saying that there is a quietness in listening. There is no registration, but most of us are not quiet.

P: We can't answer that question of yours: Why should one register?

K: No. I am asking quite a different question. Someone calls you a fool. Don't register it at all.

P: It is not a process in which I can register or I can't register. The way you put it, you are suggesting two alternatives: it is either to register or not to register.

K: No. You are registering all the time.

P: There is a registration all the time. So long as my senses are moving outward, there is registration.

K: No; when you say 'as long as', that means you are not now.

P: No. I am giving an explanation.

K: I want to find out whether this vast stream of the past can come to an end. That is all my question.

P: You won't accept anything. You won't accept any final statement on it. Therefore, there has to be a way to end.

K: I am asking: How can it end?

P: So, we have to move from that to the brain cells—to the actual registration.

K: So, the brain cells are registering. Those brain cells which are so heavily conditioned, have realized that momentum is the only safety. So, in that momentum, the brain has found tremendous security. Right?

P: Please listen to me. There is only one movement which is the movement of the past, touching the present and moving on.

K: The past meeting the present, moving on, modifying—we have gone into that. The brain is conditioned to that. It sees as long as that stream exists, it is perfectly safe. Now, how are those cells to be shown that the momentum of the past in which the brain cells have found enormous security and well-being is the most dangerous movement? Now, to point out to that brain the danger of this momentum is all that matters. The moment it sees the actual danger, it will end it. Do you see the danger of this movement? Not the theoretical danger, but the actual physical danger?

P: Are your brain cells saying that this movement is dangerous?

K: My brain is using the words to inform you of the danger, but it has no danger in it. It has seen it and dropped it. Do you see the danger of a cobra? When you see the danger, you avoid it. You avoid it because you have been conditioned through millennia to the danger of a snake. So, your responses are according to the conditioning, which is instant action.

The brain has been conditioned to carry on because in that there is complete safety, in meeting the present, learning from it, modifying it and moving on. To the brain, that is the only safe movement it knows, so it is going to remain there. But the moment the brain realizes that it is the most dangerous thing, it drops it because it wants security.

Raj: I don't see the danger of the momentum as actually as you see it.

K: Why, sir?

Raj: Partly because I have never observed the vast momentum to see its danger.

K: Are you living with the description of the momentum or living with the momentum itself which is you? You understand my question, sir? Is the momentum different from you?

Raj: No, sir.

K: So, you are the momentum? So, you are watching yourself?

Raj: Yes. But this does not happen often.

K: Often? The words 'often' and 'continuous' are awful words. Are you aware without any choice that you are the momentum, not sometimes? You can say: I only see the precipice occasionally. If the word is not the thing, then the word is not fear. Now, has the word created fear?

R: No.

K: Don't quickly answer it. Find out. Go slowly, Radhaji. The word is not the thing. That is very clear. Fear is not the word, but has the word created the fear? Without the word, would that thing called 'fear' exist? The word is the registration process. Then, something totally new arises. That new, the brain refuses because it is a new thing; so, it immediately says it is fear. For the brain to hold the momentum of that, wait, watch. Give a gap between the movement of thought, without interfering with the actual movement of feeling. The gap can only happen when you go very deeply into the question that the word is not the thing, the word is not fear. Immediately, you have stopped the momentum. I wonder if you see this.

P: I still want to get the thing clear. Is it possible to hold a quality of feeling without the word, whether it is hatred, anger or fear.

K: Of course, you can hold the feeling of anger, fear, without the word; just remain with that feeling. Do it.

P: But what do you do exactly?

K: When fear arises from whatever cause, remain with it, without any momentum, without any movement of thought.

P: What is it then?

K: It is no longer the thing which I have associated with the past as fear. I would say it is energy held without any movement. When energy is held without any movement, there is an explosion. That then gets transformed.

The Brain Cells and the Holistic State

DS: I wonder if we could discuss the question of momentum—which is the creation of the thinker and which produces the identification with the thinker? The fact is that we are faced with this momentum, this movement. Could we examine that?

P: Do you not think that in order to investigate that, one should go into the problem of dissipating energy?

DS: I don't know what you mean by that.

P: The momentum which pushes us, creates and disappears. Just as there is the engine which has energy, and which dissipates, there is the same kind of energy involved in the momentum which we are speaking about. Could we go into energy, the energy which dissipates and the energy which does not dissipate?

DS: Maxwell says, for a scientist, the first principle of energy is one of defining relationship. When you say 'energy', I am seriously asking what the problem is. I am wondering when we say 'energy', do we mean a substance, a definable force? Or, does this 'energy' imply a form of relationship?

P: I don't quite comprehend what you say.

DS: I question whether there is anyone who has actually thought about what energy is in the psychological sense.

P: That is why if we discussed it, it might clarify matters.

DS: Do we mean a substance or a force that exists within the person, or is 'energy' something that is manifested in relationship, and if so, then it raises a whole category of questions.

P: Doesn't physics (I have no knowledge of physics) accept that there is an energy which dissipates and an energy which in itself does not have the seed of dissipation?

FW: Yes, but you see, no physicist can define what energy is. Energy is a basic assumption in physics—that it is there. We know that energy is necessary. Without energy, no force is possible. Without energy, no work is possible. So, energy and work are very much related. So, we can use force, we can see work being done, but we can never see energy.

K: Is there an energy which is endless, without a beginning and without an end? And is there an energy which is mechanical which always has a motive? And is there an energy in relationship? I would like to find out.

P: Dr Shainberg asked what is it that gives momentum.

K: What is it? Let us keep to that.

P: Is momentum the arising of the thinker, and then the thinker giving himself continuity?

K: What is the drive, the force behind all our action? Is it mechanical? Or is there an energy, a force, a drive, a momentum which has no friction? Is that what we are discussing?

DS: What is the momentum of this energy that becomes mechanical? Let us stay out of the fantasy realm for a while but keep to just this momentum of thought and desire and its mechanical nature. What is the momentum of this energy, of thought, desire and the creation of the thinker?

K: Go on, sir, discuss it.

DS: You see thought, sensation, then power, then desire, and fulfilment of desire; the whole drive with a little modification goes on, continues. So, that is the momentum.

K: You are asking what is the momentum behind desire. I desire a car. What is behind that desire? We will keep it very simple. What is the urge, the drive, the force, the energy behind the desire that says, 'I must have a car'?

DS: Is it that you desire a car or does the car come up as a desire and then creates the 'I'? Is the 'I' created by desire?

K: If I didn't actually see the car, didn't feel it, didn't touch it, I would have no desire for a car. Because I see people driving in a car, the pleasure of driving, the energy, the fun of driving, I desire it.

P: Sir, is it only the object which creates desire?

DS: That is the question.

K: It may be a physical object, or a non-physical object, a belief, an idea, anything.

FW: But in the first place, it probably has to be perceivable by the senses, because you perceive something by the senses, and you make an image of it, then you desire it. So, could one say that whatever can be desired has to be sensed? And so from your question I ask: Anything which can be desired, has it first to be perceivable through the senses? One could, of course, speak of 'God'. I can desire God.

P: It is desire that maintains and keeps the world going. Can you take desire back to its roots?

DS: Would there be desire if there were no 'I'?

K: What is the momentum behind any desire? Let us begin with that. What is the energy that makes me desire? What is behind my being here? I have come here to find out what you are talking about, what this discussion is about. The desire is to discover something other than my usual rush of thought. So, what is that? Is that desire? Now, what is behind the desire that made me come here? Is it my suffering? Is it my pleasure? Is it that I want to learn more? Put all these together, what is it that is behind all that?

DS: To me it is relief from what I am.

P: Which is identical with a sense of becoming.

K: Becoming? What is behind becoming?

162

DS: To get somewhere different from where I am, and there also there is desire.

K: What is behind that energy that is making you do that? Is it punishment and reward? All our structure of movement is based on punishment and reward, to avoid one, to gain the other. Is that the basic drive or energy that is making us do so many things? So is the motive, the drive, the energy derived from these two: to avoid one and gain the other?

DS: Yes. That is part of it. That is at the level of thought.

K: No. Not at the level of thought only. I don't think so. I am hungry, my reward is food. If I do something wrong, my reward is punishment.

M: Is that different from pleasure and pain? Is reward the same as pleasure, and punishment the same as pain?

K: Reward—keep to that word. Don't enlarge that word. Reward and punishment. I think that is the basic, ordinary, common drive.

P: Reward and punishment to whom?

K: Not 'to whom'. That which is satisfactory, and that which is not satisfactory.

P: But for whom? You have to posit it.

K: I have not yet come to that. The problem is, what is satisfying I call 'reward', that which is not satisfying I call 'punishment'.

DS: Yes.

K: So, is there not the 'I' saying: 'I must be satisfied', 'I am hungry'?

P: Hunger is a very physiological thing.

K: I am keeping to that for the moment. Does the physiological spill over into the psychological field and does the whole cycle begin there? I need food; food is necessary. But that same urge goes into the field of psychology, and there begins a completely different cycle. But it is the same movement.

163

Singh: Sir, where is all this process going on? If it goes on in me, what I experience, when I participate in this process of investigation, where is it taking place? Is it in the brain? Where do I find this pleasure—pain need?

K: Both at the biological level and the psychological.

Singh: If it is the brain, then there is definitely something, which one may say is twilight, between pleasure and pain. There are definitely some moments when there is no need to satisfy hunger and still the desire to be satisfied is there. I may be satisfied and may still feel hungry.

K: I don't quite follow what you are saying.

Singh: Sir, if there is reward and punishment, and if this process of reward and punishment is to be investigated in the brain, at the physiological level, then there are some responses in the brain which are in between reward and punishment.

K: You mean there is a gap between reward and punishment?

Q: Not a gap, but an interlink, a bridge.

GM: You mean there is a state which is neither reward nor punishment?

Singh: Yes. Where one merges into another.

P: If I may ask, there may be another state, but I do not know what it is. How does this answer the question, how does this further the question of the nature of this force which brings it into being and then keeps it going? Basically, that is the question.

DS: That is the question. Where is this momentum? Where is this momentum of reward and punishment? And even if there were space in between——

K: Are you asking, what is it that is pushing one in the direction of reward and punishment? What is the energy, what is the momentum, what is the force, what is the volume of energy, that is making us do this or avoid that? Is that the question? Could it be satisfaction, gratification, which is pleasure?

DS: But then, what is gratification? What is your state of being when you are aware that there is freedom from hunger?

K: It is very simple, isn't it? There is hunger, food is given, and you are satisfied. But the same thing is carried on and it is never ending. I seek one satisfaction after another and it is endless. Is it that this energy, the drive to be satisfied, is both biological as well as psychological? I am hungry and psychologically I am lonely. There is the feeling of emptiness, there is the feeling of insufficiency. And so I turn to God, to the Church, to gurus. Physiologically, the insufficiency is satisfied very easily. Psychologically, it is never satisfied.

Par: At what point does one go from the physiological fulfilment to the thought process?

K: Sir, it may be that the physiological movement has entered into the psychological movement and carries on. Is this so?

P: What I am trying to enquire into is this: It is not a question of whether it is possible or whether it is a matter of choice. It is so from the moment I am born. Both types of wants begin. Therefore, I am asking, what is the source of both beginnings, the physiological and psychological?

Q: The one word 'insufficiency' should be enough.

P: It isn't. Both are structured in a force which then propels. That structure within one, the coming together of a number of things, is the centre, the 'I'.

K: Look. I don't think it is the 'I'.

P: What is it? Why do you say that?

K: I don't think it is the 'I'. I think it is the endless dissatisfaction, the endless insufficiency.

DS: What is the source of that?

P: Can there be insufficiency unless there is someone who is insufficient?

DS: Who is insufficient?

P: Can there be insufficiency without the one who feels it?

K: I don't posit the 'I'. There is continuous insufficiency. I go to Marxism. I find it insufficient, I go from one to the other. The more intelligent I am, the more awake I am, the more dissatisfaction there is. Then, what takes place?

S: You are implying by that, that there is a matrix without the reality of the 'I' which in its very momentum can act.

K: I don't know the matrix. I don't know the 'I'. All that I am pointing out is the one factor that there is physiological insufficiency which has entered into the field of psychological insufficiency and that goes on endlessly.

DS: There is an endless sense of incompletion.

K: Insufficiency. Keep to that word.

A: I suggest at this point that we may cut out the physiological insufficiency.

K: I am purposely insisting on that. It may be from the flowing out of that, that we create all this misery.

Par: I question that. Is it a mixture of physiological and psychological spilling over? What do we exactly mean by 'spilling over'? One is a fact, the other is not.

K: No. Therefore, there is only physiological insufficiency.

P: How can you say that?

K: I don't say that. I am just investigating.

P: There is both physiological as well as psychological insufficiency.

K: Look, Pupulji, for the moment I will not use the word 'I'. I am not investigating the 'I'. I feel hungry. It has been satisfied. I feel sexual, that is being satisfied. And I say: 'That is not good enough, I must have something more.'

166

P: The 'more'?

K: The 'more', what is that?

P: It is the momentum, isn't it?

K: No, the 'more' is more satisfaction.

P: What is the momentum then?

K: Keep to that word. The brain is seeking satisfaction.

P: Why should the brain seek satisfaction?

K: Because it needs stability; it needs security. Therefore, it says: 'I have discovered this: I thought I had found satisfaction in this but there isn't any. I shall find satisfaction and security in that, and again there isn't any'. And it keeps going on and on. That is so in daily life. I go to one guru after another, or one theory after another, one conclusion after another.

Q: Sir, the very nature of this insufficiency at a physiological level leads to sufficiency at the metaphysiological level. It leads from some inadequacy in the physiological machine to the completion of it. And it is this cycle that is operative; that is how the brain works. If the physiological spill-over is ever to continue in the psychological field, then this cycle of insufficiency and sufficiency must continue.

K: Must continue? Examine yourself. It is very simple. You are seeking satisfaction. Everybody is. If you are poor, you want to be rich. If you see somebody richer than you, you want that, somebody more beautiful, you want that and so on and on. We want continuous satisfaction.

A: Sir, I want to draw your attention again to the central feature of physiological insufficiency, that every activity to fulfil that physiological insufficiency leads to satisfaction. That is to say, between the insufficiency and its recurrence, there is always a gap, as far as the physiological insufficiency is concerned; whereas where psychological insufficiency is concerned, we begin a cycle in which we do not know any gap.

167

K: Forget the gap, sir. That is not important. Watch yourself. Isn't the whole of the movement, the energy, a drive to find gratification, reward? Shainberg, what do you say to this?

DS: I think what is coming out of this model of the physiological reward-punishment scheme is definitely so. I mean that is the whole way the 'me' functions, whether it is logical or not.

K: The whole momentum of seeking satisfaction is captured by the 'I'.

DS: Then it is there that the 'I' becomes manifest.

K: That's it. That is what I mean. I am seeking satisfaction. It never says, 'satisfaction is being sought'. I am seeking satisfaction. Actually it should be the other way: satisfaction being sought.

DS: Satisfaction sought creates the 'I'.

K: So momentum is the urge to be satisfied.

P: I will ask you a question which may seem to be a movement away. Isn't the 'I' sense inherent in the brain cells which have inherited knowledge?

K: I question that.

P: I am asking you, sir: listen to the question. The knowledge of man which is present in the brain cells, which is present in the depths of the sub-consciousness, isn't that 'I' part of the brain?

S: Pupulji, are you then equating the whole of the past with the 'I'?

P: Of course, the whole of the past. I am asking whether the 'I' comes into existence because of this manifestation of seeking satisfaction. Or, whether that very centre of memory, the matrix of memory, whether that is not the 'I' sense.

K: You are asking, is there the 'I', the 'me' the ego, identifying itself with the past, as knowledge.

P: Not identifying itself.

K: Wait. Let me get the question clear.

P: Not identifying itself. But 'I' as time, time as the past. And the 'I' sense is the whole of that.

K: Wait. You said at the beginning, does the brain contain the 'I'? I would say tentatively, investigating, there is no 'I' at all but only the search for pure satisfaction.

P: Is the whole racial memory of man fictitious?

K: No. But the moment you say I am the past that 'I' is fictitious.

S: Is the past itself saying that I am the past, or a part of the past saying that it is the past?

K: You see you are raising a question which is really very interesting: Do you observe the past as the 'I'? There is the whole past, millennia of human endeavour, human suffering, human misery, confusion, millions of years. There is only that movement that current, there is only that vast river—not 'I' and the vast river.

P: I would like to put it this way: When this vast river comes to the surface, it brings to the surface the movement of the 'I'. It gets identified with the 'I'.

Chorus: I don't think so.

K: Pupulji, the 'I' may merely be a means of communication.

DS: Is it a way of talking, reporting?

P: Is it as simple as that?

K: No, I am just stating. It is not as simple as that.

S: Sir, at one point you said the manifestation of the stream is the individual. When this vast stream of sorrow manifests itself as the individual, is the 'I' present or not?

K: Wait, wait. That is not the point. That vast stream manifests itself in this, in a human being; the father gives to me a form and then I say 'I', which is the form, the name, the idiosyncratic environment, but that stream is 'me'. There is this vast stream which is obvious.

169

A: I am saying that we are looking with our existing knowledge at the stream and identifying ourselves with the stream. The identification is done *post facto*, whereas it really starts with the momentum.

K: No, no.

P: How can one see that? You see, the way Krishnaji puts it does not really lead to the depth of oneself. The depth of oneself says, 'I want to, I will become, I will be'. That depth springs from the past, which is knowledge, which is the whole racial unconscious.

K: Can I ask, why is the 'I' there? Why do you say 'I want'? There is only want.

P: Still by saying that, you don't eliminate the 'I'.

K: No, you do eliminate that 'I'. How do you observe? In what manner do you observe this stream? Do you observe it as the 'I', observing? Or, is there observation of the stream only?

P: What one does in observing is a different issue. We are talking of that nature of energy which brings about the momentum. Now I am saying the momentum is the very nature and structure of the 'I' which is caught in becoming.

K: I want to question whether the 'I' exists at all. It may be totally verbal, non-factual. It is only a word that has become tremendously important, not the fact.

FW: Isn't there an imprint of the 'I' in the brain matter? Isn't that an actuality?

K: No, I question it.

FW: But the imprint is there. The question is: If it isn't an actuality, then what is it?

K: The whole momentum, this vast stream is in the brain. After all, that is the brain, and why should there be the 'I' at all in that?

P: When you are talking of the actual, it is there.

K: It is there only verbally.

DS: It is actually there. In the sense if you and I are together, there are two parts to it; my identification with myself is the 'I', is the relationship with you.

K: Sir, when are you conscious of the 'I'?

DS: Only in relationship.

K: I want to understand when you are conscious of the 'I'.

DS: When I want something, when I identify myself with something, or when I look at myself in the mirror.

K: When you experience, at the moment of experiencing something, there is no 'I'.

P: All right, there is no 'I'. We agree with you. But then the 'I' emerges a second later.

K: How? Look, go into it slowly.

FW: There is the question of momentum.

K: You are missing my point. There is experience. At the moment of crisis there is no 'I'. Then, later, comes the thought which says: 'That was exciting, that was pleasurable,' and that thought creates the 'I' which says: 'I have enjoyed it.' Right?

P: What has happened there? Is the 'I' a concentration of energy?

K: No.

P: The energy that dissipates?

K: It is the energy that dissipates, yes.

P: But still it is the 'I".

K: No, it is not 'I'. It is an energy that is being misused. It isn't the 'I' that uses the energy wrongly.

P: I am not saying I use the energy wrongly. The 'I' itself is a concentration of energy that dissipates. As the body wears out, the 'I' in that sense has the same nature, it gets old, it gets stale.

K: Pupul, just listen to me. At the moment of crisis, there is no 'I'. Follow it. Now can you live, is there a living at the height of that crisis, all the time? Crisis demands total energy. Crisis of any kind brings about the influx of all energy. Leave it for the moment. We will break it up afterwards. At that second, there is no 'I'. It is so.

DS: That is a movement.

K: No. At that precise second, there is no 'I'. Now, I am asking: 'Is it possible to live at that height all the time?'

DS: Why are you asking that?

K: If you don't live that way, you have all kinds of other activities which will destroy that.

DS: What is the question?

K: The point is this: the moment thought comes in, it brings about a fragmentation of energy. Thought itself is fragmentary. So, when thought enters, then it is a dissipation of energy.

DS: Not necessarily.

Par: You said: 'At the moment of experience, there is no "I".'

K: Not that 'I said'. It *is* so.

Par: Is that the momentum?

P: No. The question really amounts to this; we say it is so. But still that does not answer the question as to why the 'I' has become so powerful. You have still not answered the question even though at the moment of crisis, the 'I' is not, the whole past is not.

K: That is the point. At the moment of crisis, there is nothing.

P: Why are you saying 'no' to the 'I' being the mirror of the whole racial past?

K: I am saying 'no' because it may be merely a way of communication.

P: Is it as simple as that? Is the 'I' structure as simple as that?

172

K: I think it is extraordinarily simple. What is much more interesting, much more demanding, is that whenever thought comes into being, then dissipation of energy begins. So, I say to myself: 'Is it possible to live at that height?' The moment the 'I' comes into being, there is dissipation. If you left out the 'I' and I left out the 'I', then we would have right relationship.

FW: You said the moment thought comes in, there is dissipation of energy. But the moment the 'I' comes in, there is also dissipation of energy. What is the difference?

K: Thought is memory, experience, all that.

FW: You have to use it in your life.

DS: Which is just what we are doing right now. I find when I say dissipation of energy, I immediately see myself take up the position of the observer and say 'that is bad'. What I am suggesting is that you can be neutrally aware. There is a crisis and a dissipation, a crisis and a dissipation. That is the flow of existence.

K: No.

P: K's point is, there is that, but the transformation which we are talking about is to negate that.

DS: I question whether there is any such thing as breaking out of this. I think we remember the intensity of the energy of the crisis, and then we say I would like to keep it all the time. Do you do that?

K: No.

DS: Then why ask the question?

K: I am asking that question purposely because thought interferes.

DS: Not all the time.

K: No. All the time. Question it, sir. The moment you have a crisis, there is no past, nor present, only that moment. There is no time in that crisis. The moment time comes in, dissipation begins. Keep it for the minute like that.

173

A: There is the crisis. Then, there is dissipation and then identification.

P: At the moment of crisis, many things happen. You talk of a holistic position at the moment of crisis. Even to come to that, one has to investigate it very deeply, in oneself in order to know what this thing is.

K: You see Pupul holistic implies a very sane mind and body, a clear capacity to think, and also it means holy, sacred; all that is implied in that word 'holistic'. Now, I am asking: 'Is there an energy which is never dissipated, which you want to draw from?' There is dissipation when it is not holistic. A holistic way of life is one in which there is no dissipation of energy. A non-holistic way of living in dissipation of energy.

P: What is the relationship of the holistic and the non-holistic to the brain cells?

K: There is no relationship to the brain cells. Let us look at it. I want to be quite clear that we understand the meaning of that word 'holistic'. It means complete, whole, harmony, no disintegration, no fragmentation. That is the holistic life. That is endless energy. The non-holistic life, the fragmented life, is a wastage of energy. When there is a feeling of the whole, there is no 'I'. The other is the movement of thought, of the past, of time; that is our life, our daily life, and that life is reward and punishment and the continuous search for satisfaction.

P: Sir, the holistic is held in the brain cells. That is, it throws up responses, challenges. The non-holistic is held in the brain cells. It is the whole stream of the past meeting the challenge. Now, what relationship has the holistic to the brain cells and the senses?

K: Have you understood the question, Doctor?

DS: Her question is: What is the relationship of this holistic state in the brain to memory and the past and the senses?

K: No, no. You haven't listened.

P: I said there are two states, the holistic and the non-holistic. The non-holistic is definitely held in the brain cells because it is the stream of the past held in the brain cells, challenged and giving momentum. I am asking what is the relationship of the holistic to the brain cells and to the senses?

DS: What do you mean by the senses?

P: Listening, seeing, tasting . . .

DS: Can I go into that? I think if there were something in what we were saying, there would be a different relationship of such part functions in the holistic state. They are not merely part functioning but functioning as part of the holistic state, whereas in the dissipation of energy and fragmentation, it begins to function as isolated centres.

K: Sir, her question is very simple. Our brain cells now contain the past, memory, experience, knowledge of millennia, and those brain cells are not holistic.

DS: Yes, they are separate cells.

K: They are not holistic. Stick to that. She says the brain cells now are conditioned to a non-holistic way of living. What takes place in the brain cells when there is a holistic way? That is her question.

DS: I would put it differently. I would say: 'What takes place in the relationship to the brain cells in the holistic state of perception?'

K: I am going to answer that question. Does the holistic brain contain the past and therefore can the past be used holistically? Because it is whole, it contains the part, but the part cannot contain the whole. Therefore, when there is the operation of the part, there is dissipation of energy.

P: After going through all this, we have come to this point.

K: Yes. A marvellous point. Stick to it.

P: What is then its place in the brain which is the structure of the human mind?

K: We know only the non-holistic way of living, keep to that. That is the fact, that we live non-holistically, fragmentarily. That is our actual life and that is a wastage of energy. We see also that there is contradiction, there is battle. All that is a wastage of energy. Now, we are asking: 'Is there a way of living which is not a wastage of energy?'

We live a non-holistic way of life, a fragmentary life, a broken life. You understand what I mean by broken, saying something, doing something else, a life that is contradictory, comparative, imitative, conforming, having moments of silence. It is a fragmentary way of living, a non-holistic way, that is all we know. And somebody says: Is there an energy which is not wasted? And with that question let us investigate it to see if it is possible to end this way of living.

P: But I have asked another question, and you have still not answered that.

K: I am coming to that. That is a very difficult question to answer which is: one lives a non-holistic life, which is a constant seepage of energy, a wastage of energy. The brain is conditioned to that. One sees that actually. Then one asks: Is it possible to live a life which is not that? Right?

Q: Not always, sir, that is what we are investigating. Whether that breath of freedom could be a totality.

K: No, it can never be totality, because it comes and goes. Anything that comes and goes involves time. Time involves a fragmentary way of living. Therefore, it is not whole. Look we live a non-holistic life. The brain is conditioned to that. Occasionally, I may have a flair of freedom but that flair of freedom is still within the field of time. Therefore, that flair is still a fragment. Now, can the brain that is conditioned to that, a non-holistic way of living, can that brain so completely transform itself that it no longer lives the way of conditioning? That is the question.

DS: My response to that is: Here you are in a state of fragmentation; here you are in a state of dissipation of energy. And there you are looking for satisfaction.

K: No, I am not. I am saying this is a wastage of energy.

DS: That is all we know and nothing else.

K: Yes. Nothing else. So, the brain says: 'All right, I see that.' Then it asks the question: 'Is it possible to change all this?'

DS: I wonder whether the brain can ask it.

K: I am asking it. Therefore, if one brain asks it, the other brain must ask it too. This is not based on satisfaction.

DS: Could you say anything about how you can ask the question about what you state without seeking satisfaction?

K: It can be asked because the brain has realized for itself the game it has been playing.

DS: So, how is the brain to raise the question?

K: It is asking it, because it says, 'I am seeing through that.' Now, it says: 'Is there a way of living which is non-fragmentary, which is holistic?'

DS: And that question is as holistic as any.

K: No, not yet.

DS: That is what I am having trouble with—where that question comes from. You say it is not seeking satisfaction, it is not holistic. Then, what brain is producing this question?

K: The brain which says: 'I see very clearly the waste of energy'.

P: The very fact of your saying that the brain is seeing through the whole problem of fragmentation . . .

K: Is the ending of it.

P: Is that holistic?

K: The ending of it, that is holistic.

P: The ending is the very seeing of fragmentation.

DS: Is that holistic?

K: That is holistic. But she asked a much more complex question in regard to the holistic brain which contains the past, the totality of the past, the essence of the past, the juice of it, sucking in everything of the past. What does that mean? The past is nothing, but such a brain can use the past. I wonder if you follow this. My concern is with one's life, actual, daily, fragmentary, stupid life. And I say, 'Can that be transformed?' Not into greater satisfaction. Can that structure end itself? Not by an imposition of something higher which is just another trick. I say if you are capable of observing without the observer, the brain can transform itself. That is meditation. Sir, the essence is the whole. In fragmentation, there is no essence of anything.

Listening with the Heart

P: I feel the central point missing in all of us is the factor of compassion. In Benaras, you once used a phrase, 'Is it possible to listen with the heart?' What does it imply to listen with the heart?

K: Shall we discuss that?

FW: Could we enquire into the nature of matter?

K: You see, sir, what I said was that thought is a material process and whatever thought has built—technological, psychological beliefs, the gods, the whole structure of religion based on thought, is a material process. Thought in that sense is matter. Thought is experience, knowledge stored up in the cells and functioning in a particular groove set by knowledge. All that to me is a material process. What matter is, I do not know. I won't even discuss that because I don't know.

FW: I am not enquiring into it from the point of view of a scientist. Let me say matter is something unknown. So I feel when we explore into the unknown . . .

K: You can't explore into the unknown. Be careful, you can explore into the known, go to the limit of it and when you come to the limit of it you have moved out of it. You can only enquire into the known.

P: Which is, into thought?

K: Of course. But when he says examine, explore, investigate into the unknown, we can't. So Pupul puts a question which is: What is it, what does it mean to listen with compassion?

P: This is a crucial thing. If we have compassion, everything is.

179

K: Agreed, but we have not got it, unfortunately. So how should we approach this matter? What does it mean to listen, and what is the nature and the structure of compassion?

P: And what is this listening with the heart? It is a very important thing. Is there a listening which is much deeper than the ear listening?

K: Can we take the two: listening and listening with the heart, with compassion. First, what does it mean to listen, what is the art of listening?

FW: Perhaps we could approach the subject the other way round. What does it mean *not* to listen?

K: What do you mean, sir?

FW: When we ask what does it mean to listen, it seems very difficult and I think that perhaps if I am very clear about what it means not to listen . . .

K: It is the same thing. That is, through negation come to the positive. If you could find out what is listening and in the investigation of what is listening you negate what is *not* listening, then you are listening. That is all.

P: Can we go on? So there are two problems involved, which are, what is listening—in which is implied what is not listening—and what is compassion? What is the nature and the structure of the feeling and the depth of it, and the action that springs from it?

K: Go on, discuss it.

FW: I feel that in this question of compassion we have the same problem, because I feel that compassion has nothing to do with the field of the known.

K: She meant something else, sir. What does it mean to listen with your heart? That was what she meant. I introduced the word 'compassion'. Perhaps we can leave that out for the moment.

P: Krishnaji spoke of a listening with the heart, and I am interested in going into that.

K: So let us keep to those two: listening, and listening with one's heart, what does it mean?

R: We have said that the response with thought is fragmentary. Whether we call that response observation or listening or whatever it is, it is the same thing. Isn't it? So is the heart the non-fragmentary? Is that what we mean?

K: Now wait a minute. To listen with the total flowering of all senses is one thing; listening partially with a particular sense is fragmentary.

R: Yes.

K: That is, if I listen with all my senses, then there is no problem of negation of what is listening or not listening. But we do not listen.

S: Sir, when you talk of listening with the heart, my response is I do not know it. But there is a movement, a feeling, a listening in which consciousness is not thought. I see that there is a movement of feeling when I listen to Radhaji or someone; there is a certain feeling with which one listens to another. There is a different kind of communication when that feeling is there.

K: Is feeling different from thought?

S: That is what I am coming to.

P: It is different from thought.

S: If feeling is not different from thought, we do not know any movement apart from that of thought. To accept that statement is very difficult because we have also experienced tenderness, affection. If everything is put in the category of thought, if it is the totality of consciousness then . . .

K: We must be clear. Do not categorize it. Let us go slowly. Do I listen with thought or do I not listen with thought? That is the problem.

S: Both are . . .

K: Go slowly Sunanda. Do you listen with the movement of thought or do you listen without the movement of thought? I am asking you.

P: Can we listen without thought?

K: Yes.

P: Sometimes, once in a lifetime may be, one gets the total feeling of the heart and the mind and consciousness being one.

K: I understand that.

P: When we ask if there is a listening without thought, we can say, 'Yes, it is so'; but if I may say so, there is something still lacking.

K: We will come to that. Let us go slowly into this.

A: At a lower voltage of sensitivity there may be no articulated thought, but there is listening. That listening is lacking in sensitivity. So it is not alive.

K: I think we have to begin with what it means to communicate. I want to tell you something which I am deeply concerned with. You must be prepared to enter into the problem, or into the question, or into the statement which one is proposing; which means you must have the same interest as the speaker or the same intensity, and also meet him at the same level. All this is implied in communication. Otherwise there is no communication.

S: Interest one can understand, but level is very difficult to know.

P: May I say something? In introducing the word 'communication', you are introducing the two. In listening from the heart there may not be the two.

K: Yes. We will come to that. What is listening with one's heart? I want to tell you something which I feel profoundly. How do you listen to it? I want you to share it with me, I want you to feel it with me, I want you to be involved with me. Otherwise how can there be communication?

S: How does one know the level?

K: The moment it is not intellectual, verbal, but an intense problem, a burning problem, a deep, human problem that I want to convey to you, to share with you. Then we must be on the same level, otherwise you cannot listen.

S: If there is deep seriousness, will the right level be there?

K: You are not listening now. That is my problem. I want to tell you something which is profoundly important. I want you to listen to it because you are a human being and it is your problem. It may be you have not really delved into it. So, in sharing it with me, you are exposing your own intensity to it. Therefore listening implies a sharing, a non-verbal communication. There must be a listening, there must be a sharing, which implies an absence of verbal distortion.

P: Obviously you can only communicate if there is a certain level.

K: That is what I am saying. Now Sunanda how will you listen to me? Will you listen like that?

S: It seems that one does not listen like that to everyone.

K: I am talking now, I am asking you, will you listen to me in that manner?

P: To you we listen.

K: Because you have built an image about me and that image you give importance to, and therefore you listen.

S: Not to the image alone.

K: You are missing my point. Can you not only listen to this man who is speaking at the moment, but also listen to Radha when she talks about it, or when Parchure or you or somebody says something? Can you listen? He may convey something to you which he may not be capable of putting into words? So will you, in the same manner, listen to all of us?

S: We listen to some and we do not listen to all.

K: Why?

P: Because of prejudice.

K: Of course. There, there is no communication.

P: You mean to say, sir, listening to the voice which is established in truth and which speaks out of silence, the receiving of that, can it be the same as listening to the voice which speaks out of thought? Please answer that question.

K: You are too definite.

P: No, it is not too definite. When you speak, your voice is different.

R: I think the point is whether there is a receiving at all, listening at all. If one is receiving, then the question of whether it is the voice of truth or something else does not arise.

P: It does not happen with us.

Raj: We listen with motive. The motive may be very subtle or very obvious. When we listen to another we think we will not get anything out of it. That is why, when we listen to K there is much more attention.

K: So how do we alter all that and listen to each other?

FW: Is it that we interpret?

K: No, don't interpret what I am saying, for God's sake, listen. I go to Kata and tell him I know nothing about Karate. I watch it on the films but I don't know Karate. So I go to him now, not knowing. Therefore I am listening. But we *know*—and that is your difficulty. You say this should be this way, this should be that way—all conjectures, opinions. The moment I use a word, you are fully alive. But the first thing is the art of listening. Art means to put everything in its right place. You may have your prejudices, you may have your conclusions, but when you are listening put them away—the interpreting, comparing, judging, evaluating, put all that away. Then communication takes place. When somebody says 'I love you,' you don't say, 'Let me think about it.'

R: That is, putting away everything is the same as having the same intensity and being at the same level.

K: Otherwise what is the point of it?

R: I have seen this but I am not doing it.

K: Do it now.

S: It seems to me, you are saying the act of listening wipes away, swallows up the whole thing for the time being.

K: When I say, 'I love you,' what happens?

S: But no one says that to us.

K: But I am saying it to you.

S: No, sir, in normal life it does not often happen like that.

K: So what is the art of listening, what does it mean to listen with one's heart? If you do not listen with the heart, there is no meaning to it. If you listen with a sense of care, attention, affection, a deep sense of communion with each other, it means, you listen with all your senses, does it not?

P: With fullness.

K: Will you listen that way? Can we listen to somebody whom we don't like, who we think is stupid? Can you listen with your heart to that man or to that woman? I don't think, when you have that feeling, words matter any more.

Let us proceed. Then what? Suppose I listen and I have done it often in my life. I listen very carefully, I have no prejudices, I have no pictures, I have no conclusions, I am not a politician, I am a human being listening to somebody. I just listen, because he wants to tell me something about himself. Because he has got an image, a picture of me, he generally comes to see me with a mask. If he wants to talk seriously with me, I say 'Remove the mask, let us look at it together.' I don't want to look behind the mask unless he invites me. If he says 'All right, sir, let us talk about it,' I listen; and in listening he tells me something which is so utterly, completely common to all human beings. He may put it wrongly, he may put it foolishly, but it is something which every man or woman suffers, and he is telling me about it and I listen. Therefore he is telling me the history of mankind. So I am listening not only to the words, the superficial feeling of his, but also to the profound depth of what he is saying. If it is superficial, then we discuss superficially and push it till he feels this thing profoundly. You follow? It may be that he is expressing a feeling which is very superficial and if it is superficial, I say let us go a little deeper. So in going deeper and deeper, he is expressing something which is totally common to all of us. He is expressing something which so completely belongs to all human beings. You understand? So there is no division between him and me.

P: What is the source of that listening?

K: Compassion. So, what is compassion? As Fritz says, it is unknown to us. So how am I to have that extraordinary intelligence which is compassion? I would like to have that flower in my heart. Now what is one to do?

FW: Compassion is not in the field of thought. Therefore I can never have the feeling that I have it.

K: No, you won't find it—it is like a drill, like a screwdriver, you have to push, push.

P: There must be a perfume to it.

K: Of course. You cannot talk about compassion without perfume, without honey.

P: It is either there or not there. Why is it then, sir, that when we are in communication with you we have this feeling, why is it that you have this tremendous impact which knocks away all prejudices, all obstacles and this immediately makes the mind silent?

K: It is like going to the well with a small bucket or with an enormous bucket which one can hardly carry. Most of us go with a small bucket and pull out of the well insufficient water. It is like having a fountain in your yard, flowing, flowing. I would like to watch it, see it out there and inside. So what am I to do?

FW: I will find out what prevents me from having that.

K: That is analysis. I won't analyse, because it is a waste of time. I have understood that, not because I have said it and you have accepted it, but I see the reason, the logic, the significance and therefore the truth of it. Therefore analysis is out.

S: Not only that, sir, I also see that sitting in meditation regularly, being in silence, none of these things have any relationship to that. Duality and every kind of experience that one has gone through, has also nothing to do with it.

K: Listen Sunanda, Radha and Pupul have got this thing in their backyard. They don't talk about it because it is there, flowering, flowing, murmuring, all kinds of things happen. And I say, Why is it not in my backyard? I want to find out. Not that I want to imitate. But it must happen. I won't analyse what prevents me, what blocks me, I won't ask, should I be silent, should I not be silent? That is the analytical process. I don't know if you understand this?

S: That is clear, sir.

K: Do you really understand what it means?

S: What does it mean, 'to really understand'?

K: Look, they have got it, I haven't got it. I would like to have it. I would like to look at it like at a precious jewel. How is it to happen to me? That is my enquiry. He suggested that I look at what is blocking me. He said that is an analytical process and analysis is a waste of time. I don't know if you see that actually. Analysis and the analyser are both the same. Don't take time over it, don't meditate about it, sit cross-legged and all that. You have no time. Now, can you stop analysis? Totally? Can you do it? You do it when there is a tremendous crisis. You have no time then to analyse, you are in it. Are you in this? Do you understand my question? That is, she has got that extraordinary perfume which is

187

so natural to her. She doesn't say, 'How did I get it, what am I to do with it?' She has got it somehow, and I would like to have it. I am a human being and without it nothing matters. So it must be there. And I see the truth about analysis, therefore I will never analyse. Because I am in the middle of this question, I am soaked, burning with the question. The house is on fire and I am caught in that fire.

R: Sir, the moment the beauty of the thing exists somewhere, the question does not arise, How am I to have it?

K: I want it, how am I to have it? I do not care, I am hungry. You do not analyse hunger.

R: I am not saying that.

K: Sorry, what were you saying?

R: I am saying that when at a certain moment one is filled with this, 'I want it' does not arise. I do not know to what extent one is filled with the perfume, but this feeling, 'I want it' does not exist there.

K: You may be filled by my words, by my intensity, and then say you have got it.

R: I do not say I have got it, but . . .

K: Be simple, Radha. You have something in your backyard, a fountain which very few people have, very very few. They may talk about the water, they may talk about the beauty of the fountain, the song and the water, but that is not it. But you have got it. And as a human being, I see how marvellous that is and I go towards it, not that I want it; I go towards it, I don't have it. What am I do to?

FW: Is there anything I can do?

K: May be or may be not. May be the demand is so great I put everything aside. The demand itself puts everything aside. You understand? The house is burning. There is no argument, there is no weighing which bucket to use, which pump to use.

P: Is it not very closely linked up with the volume of energy?

188

K: All right. She says it is linked up with the flame of energy. No, Pupul, when you want something you burn like hell. Doesn't one? When you want that girl or that man, you are at it.

FW: That makes the difference.

K: I want to create a crisis. Then there is action. Do you understand what I am saying? Either you avoid the crisis or you act. Pupul, is the crisis taking place? Because it is a very important question. I come to you and talk about all this. You listen as far as you can listen, as far as you can go, but nothing happens. You hear it year after year, you take a little step each time, and by the end you are dead. What he wants to do is to bring about an action which is born out of tremendous crisis. He wants to break it up because then there is no argument, there is no analysis. He has created a crisis. Is that crisis the result of his influence, his words, his feeling, his urgency or is it a crisis which you have got to break through? That is his intention. He says that is the only thing that matters.

A: The crisis is an external challenge to which I am unable to find an adequate internal response, and because I cannot find an adequate internal response, there is this crisis. The other crisis which I understood you to speak of is not at all triggered by any external fact but it is a projection from within.

K: His intention is to create a crisis, not superficial, not external but inside.

A: Are not these two channels distinct? When the mind is seeking an external crisis and seeking an adequate response from within, that is one type of crisis; and the other type of crisis is that within you there is the deep sense of inadequacy which says that this cannot be put away because it is a heavy responsibility.

K: He has created that crisis in you, he is talking of truth. Is there a crisis when you talk to him? His demand is that there should be a crisis in you, not a superficial crisis. I think that is listening with the heart. He has turned you inwards so deeply, or he has taken away all anchorage. I think that is listening with the heart. The

189

monsoon says to you: 'Please collect all the water you can, next year there will be no monsoon.' You understand? That makes you build every kind of hold to collect water. So where are we at the end of it?

P: In a strange way it also implies lifting your hands off everything.

K: It may not. It may mean that an action which you have not pre-meditated may take place. If there is crisis, then it will happen.